T0294106

Also available at all good book stores

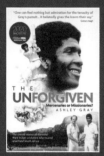

9781785315329

9781785317330

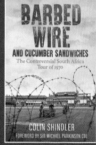

9781785316340

9781908051929

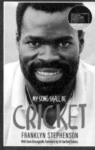

9781785315398

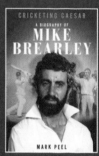

9781785316623

9781785316876

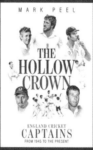

9781785316630

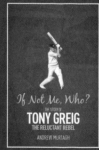

9781785316418

Kings
in
Waiting

THOMAS BLOW

Kings in Waiting

First published by Pitch Publishing, 2021

Pitch Publishing
A2 Yeoman Gate
Yeoman Way
Worthing
Sussex
BN13 3QZ
www.pitchpublishing.co.uk
info@pitchpublishing.co.uk

ISBN 978 1 78531 830 6

Typesetting and origination by Pitch Publishing
Printed and bound in India by Replika Press Pvt. Ltd.

Contents

Acknowledgements   9

Prologue: Cricket's Great Bridesmaids   11

1.   2010: Never Been Closer   17

2.   2012: End of an Era   67

3.   2016: Rogers's Resurgence   116

4.   2018: Coming of Age   163

5.   2019: The Sweetest Victory   200

Epilogue: Can Somerset Win the
Championship during the 2020s?   239

Appendix: Somerset during the 2010s   253

About the Author   254

To Eloise, for putting up with me
for five years and counting.

Acknowledgements

YOU ALWAYS need help when writing a book. Thanks as ever to my family and friends for their unconditional support – especially my partner Eloise, who is always there for me. Last year was hard for everyone, but I would not have survived it without her love and encouragement. Thanks also to her family for housing us when we escaped London just as the Covid-19 pandemic was beginning to take hold.

Thanks to everyone who bought or read my first book, *The Honorary Tyke*, and shared their thoughts. Your feedback is priceless. I also appreciate everyone who gave their opinion on the idea for this book, its structure and the manuscript.

Completing it would not have been possible without interviewing many people connected with Somerset. Thanks to Jim Allenby, Alex Barrow, Michael Bates, Nick Compton, Ryan Davies, Adam Dibble, George Dockrell, Andy Hurry, Jason Kerr, Steve Kirby, Phil Lewis, Matt Maynard, Michael Munday, Johann Myburgh, Chris Rogers, Dave Stiff, Arul Suppiah, Paul van Meekeren, Darren Veness, Andy Walter and Charl Willoughby for speaking to me. I feel humbled and privileged to work which such great people.

There are some great digital archives that have allowed me to conduct hours of precious research. Thanks to the BBC, ESPNcricinfo, *The Guardian*, the *Somerset County Gazette* and others for allowing the public to freely access articles from their respective websites. We need to stop taking free-to-read journalism for granted. It is also important to acknowledge Cricket Archive, a dream for anyone obsessed with looking at old scorecards.

Thanks to Paul and Jane at Pitch Publishing for turning this project into a reality – it has been a pleasure working with you. Sports journalism is thriving at the moment and Pitch Publishing deserve plenty of credit for their invaluable contribution to the industry. Thanks also to Duncan Olner for designing the cover and to Richard Whitehead for proofing the manuscript.

Finally, thanks to Somerset for entertaining a whole generation of county cricket fans. I hope this book does your recent history justice.

Thomas Blow, Spring 2021

Prologue
Cricket's Great Bridesmaids

THE COUNTY Championship celebrated its 130th anniversary in 2020. During that time Somerset, a team based in the small town of Taunton, have strived in 119 editions of the competition, missing only the inaugural season in 1890. That means they have had 119 chances to become Kings of England. As of spring 2021, they have failed to take any of those. Along with Northamptonshire and Gloucestershire, they are one of only three counties to have never won the Championship, although Gloucestershire were named England's 'Champion County' four times before the competition officially began in 1890.

Somerset's first-class history began in 1882, when they played their maiden match against Lancashire. While historic, it was not a pleasant occasion as they were humbled at Old Trafford. After restricting Lancashire to a modest 237, they were bowled out for 29 and 51, losing by an innings and 157 runs. They did pick up their first win later that summer, beating Hampshire by five wickets at Taunton. But it was a tough start to first-class cricket. They managed to win just five of their first 27 games between

1882 and 1885. After losing by nine wickets to W.G. Grace's Gloucestershire in 1885, they did not play first-class cricket again until 1891 when they entered the Championship. There were early flirtations with the title, finishing third in their second season. They were helped in 1892 by captain Herbie Hewett, who scored 1,047 runs at an average of 40.26. No one scored more in the Championship that season and just two had a better average. Hewett was named as one of *Wisden's* Cricketers of the Year in the following Almanack and looked to be the man to lead Somerset for years to come, but he departed in 1893 after refusing to play on a sodden pitch.

Two years later, Somerset suffered the biggest defeat in their history, losing by an innings and 452 runs to Lancashire. It was a memorable match for England's Archie MacLaren, who scored a record 424. It remained the highest first-class score in England until Warwickshire's Brian Lara hit 501 not out against Durham in 1994. To this day only Hampshire and Sussex have suffered bigger defeats in Championship cricket. It was a result which symbolised their struggles during the coming years. They failed to keep up with the likes of Surrey, Yorkshire and Lancashire, all of whom had become accustomed to winning the title. It took them more than 50 years to finish as high as third again, in 1958. Despite this, Somerset fans still saw many talented players come and go during the first half of the 20th century. Perhaps the greatest was England's Jack White. The all-rounder, who played in 15 Tests, scored more than 11,000 runs and claimed 2,165 wickets in first-class cricket for the club. No one has more of the latter for Somerset. There was also Harold Gimblett, who is their leading run-scorer in first-class cricket with 21,142 runs, and Arthur Wellard, who took more than 1,500 first-class wickets.

In the 1970s, Somerset became more consistent. The emergence of talents such as Brian Rose, Vic Marks and Ian Botham, as well as the arrivals of Brian Close, Joel Garner and Viv Richards, transformed the club into one of the best in the land. Honours followed, with both the John Player League and Gillette Cup won in 1979, the NatWest Trophy four years later, and two Benson and Hedges Cups picked up in 1981 and 1982. After failing to win any major trophies before 1979, they now had five in their cabinet thanks to a talented squad. Yet the all-important Championship title continued to evade them as they failed to break into the top two. The departures of Garner, Richards and Botham in the mid-1980s signalled the end of that great team and the opportunity to win the Championship.

Somerset did eventually finish as runners-up, coming second to Yorkshire in 2001. But with three fewer wins, they were well beaten to the title. And the following season they were relegated from Division One, leaving them a long way from breaking their duck. Their misery was compounded in 2005 as they finished eighth in Division Two. And things got even worse 12 months later as they finished rock bottom. But as they say, once you have hit the bottom, the only way is up. In January 2007, they made an appointment that triggered their return to the top. Justin Langer, the Australia opener who had just retired from Test cricket and had already agreed to join the club that summer, was named their new captain.

Since then Somerset have come very close to winning the Championship on several occasions. They finished as runners-up five times in the 2010s, metaphorically having one hand on the trophy at times. Not only that, but since they won the Twenty20 Cup in 2005, they have finished as runners-up in 12 major tournaments at the time of writing in 2020. This has led to them being described as the bridesmaids of English cricket, consistently playing a starring role in the ceremony but never being the centre of attention. In this respect the past 15 seasons have been hard. They have had to endure defeat on so many occasions, with the press labelling them as chokers. For the likes of Marcus Trescothick, Peter Trego and James Hildreth – all three of whom played for the club throughout this period, with the latter still part of the squad – they have had to live with a drawerful of runners-up medals at home, reminding them of what could have been.

Another way of looking at it, however, is recognising how brilliant they have been since Langer's appointment. Although his great side – which Trescothick inherited after his retirement in October 2009 – never managed to win a trophy, they entertained county fans across the country by playing some fabulous cricket. They challenged in every competition thanks to the brilliance of their squad. Craig Kieswetter and Jos Buttler were England's most exciting wicketkeeper-batsmen, Zander de Bruyn, Alfonso Thomas, Charl Willoughby and Murali Kartik were former internationals who were far better than your average county professional and, most importantly, they had Trescothick – still one of the best openers in the world despite his premature retirement from international cricket, caused by a well-documented stress-related illness. It was a team that could have, and should have, won countless honours.

That squad gradually disintegrated following Rose's departure as director of cricket in 2012. But a new team soon began to emerge. After Chris Rogers, in his only season as captain, inspired them to a second-place Championship finish in 2016, Tom Abell, a 22-year-old from Taunton, inherited the captaincy. Despite his age, Abell became the focal point of a brilliant team, one which remains in place today. With talents such as George Bartlett, Lewis Gregory, Tom Banton, Jack Leach and Craig Overton just entering their peak, the club's future looks very bright. And following their win in the 2019 One-Day Cup, they have finally made it to the altar. It was a nice way to finish off the decade and Trescothick's career as he retired after 27 years as a professional. But with that first Championship trophy still missing from their cabinet, it was not the way they would have wanted to conclude the 2010s.

And that is why Somerset and their quest to win the Championship is the great enigma of county cricket. They built two great teams and consistently challenged for honours. Never, not even in the years of Botham and his colleagues, had they been so consistent. But because they have failed to get over the line so many times, they are not considered as one of the best teams of the decade. They do not share the limelight with Yorkshire's back-to-back title-winning side and Essex's all-conquering team. And they are not mentioned in the same breath as the great team of the late 1970s and early 1980s, a time still regarded as Somerset's golden era.

This leaves us with so many questions. Why were they not able to win even a handful of the finals? What made them so competitive in all formats? How have they managed to produce so many young, talented players? Why could they not get over the line in the Championship? And, most importantly of all, can they win the Championship during the 2020s? All these questions will be answered during the next five chapters – centred around Somerset's five second-place finishes in the Championship – and an epilogue at the end, dedicated to that last question. So, sit back, open a cold Somerset cider and enjoy a comprehensive review of the last decade at Taunton.

2010

Never Been Closer

THERE WERE some big changes at Somerset ahead of the 2010 season. Their skipper, Justin Langer, had recently retired. A crucial part of Australia's all-conquering side of the 2000s with 23 Test centuries, Langer was a legend of the game. He joined Somerset in 2006 and became club captain a year later. And he went on to have a wonderful career at Taunton. He scored more than 3,000 first-class runs for the club at an average of 51.23, including a record-breaking knock of 342 against Surrey in July 2006. It remains the highest first-class score by a Somerset player.

Yet Langer was not just about the runs. Alongside director of cricket Brian Rose and head coach Andy Hurry, he transformed the club. Influenced by his time playing in one of cricket's greatest teams, he made Somerset winners, instilling a culture of working tirelessly to become the best you can be. Under his leadership, they rose from the foot of the second tier in 2006 to third in Division One in 2009. The county also became a force in white-ball cricket, finishing as runners-up in the final edition of the Pro 40

League and losing the Twenty20 Cup Final to Sussex in 2009. 'I love Somerset – it has been an awesome project,' he said shortly before announcing his retirement in 2009.

Langer's influence at Taunton was felt by leg-spinner Michael Munday, who, having joined the squad in 2005 before Langer arrived, was able to appreciate what he brought to the job. 'I think it's pretty safe to say there was a big change,' recalled Munday. 'I think among the committee and leadership at the club it was said, "This isn't good enough. There needs to be a real change in culture." And that's where the appointment of Langer as captain came from. There was definitely a culture shift from the first couple of games I played, where there was a very relaxed atmosphere. Ian Blackwell was my captain in my first match. He's a terrific player – naturally talented – however, he's not what you would probably consider the type of player you would want as a role model for younger players, in terms of his general approach to fitness and training. Whereas it was then very much, "Right, Langer's here" … An away trip isn't an excuse for a four-day piss-up and have a few drinks every night, it's a serious thing where we're going to prepare professionally to win games of cricket. And if people step out of line, there are going to be consequences.'

Arul Suppiah, who scored 1,201 first-class runs at an average of 48.04 in 2009, also appreciates Langer's influence. He recognises how Langer had the leadership skills to encourage the squad to follow his high standards. 'It became more professional in terms of how we trained, what we ate, where we stayed,' admitted Suppiah. 'We even took into account how much travelling we were doing. Everything was really detailed. We called it the one-per-centers, so making sure we took care of the little things and then eventually looking at the bigger picture. That was the difference. We knew the one-per-centers, that was already there, but Langer made sure we did it rather than just pay lip service to it. He was the man to lead by example. Fitness wise, he would go out and do everything first. Then we would go, "Okay, let's do it – our captain is out there." His work ethic was second to none. It was amazing.'

The culture Langer had helped instil was immediately recognised by fast bowler Dave Stiff when he joined the club in 2008. Although he was aged just 23, Stiff was experienced. He had been at Yorkshire – the county of his birth – Kent and Leicestershire before joining Somerset. 'Under the leadership of Justin Langer, it was definitely one of the more forward-thinking clubs, not just physically but tactically,' said Stiff. 'The whole outlook was more attacking than a lot of the other counties I'd been at, where it was more traditional … We had a good balance, leading on from the ethos and cutting-edge that Justin Langer had installed in the team. That really put us in a good place. There were no excuses, an honesty that he brought. Some people who played around him might have thought that he was just needlessly hard, but I found him very fair. As long as he thought everybody was giving 100 per cent, he would back them completely. Once everyone realised that was what he was all about, then it was a really great place to be.'

A key part of Langer's ideology was his desire to play an attacking brand of cricket. Fortunately, they had the talent to do so. James Hildreth, one of the finest stroke-players in county cricket, epitomised that. After making his Championship debut in 2003, Hildreth was one of the team's most prolific batsmen, having scored more than

900 first-class runs in each of the previous three summers. He was elegant, talented and exciting – a true gem in the middle order. And so was Peter Trego. The all-rounder had left Somerset in 2003 to join Kent, leaving a year later with just one first-class appearance. He then spent the summer of 2004 playing in Worcestershire's second team before moving to Middlesex in 2005. He eventually made his way back to Somerset in 2006 and became an integral part of their squad, scoring 836 runs and taking 33 wickets in first-class cricket during the promotion-winning season in 2007.

A huge part of Trego's success was Langer, who he continues to credit. 'Because I'm all bravado, tattoos and hair dye, I think people have always felt like putting the boot in is the best way of dealing with me,' wrote Trego in the December 2019 issue of *The Cricketer*. 'But JL's ability as a man manager knew somehow that I was crying out for someone to say "well done" every now and then, and the result was a Pete Trego that would run through the proverbial brick wall for his captain and his team.'

As well as attacking batsmen, Somerset also had attacking bowlers. One of them was Stiff, who was given a licence to strike by Langer. 'The captaincy of Justin Langer suited me down to the ground,' he said. 'In Championship cricket, most of the captains I came across had this feeling of, "Let's just consolidate, don't get out and don't go for runs when you're bowling." And that was almost the opposite with Langer. He had the attitude of, "Set attacking fields and just get wickets." Obviously, he didn't want to give away runs needlessly, but he came with a mindset of trying to win games.'

Having that attitude was crucial to them becoming a force in county cricket. Yet so was Langer's desire to help his colleagues improve. 'I remember he wrote everyone a letter at the end of the season, I think it was 2008,' recalled Suppiah. 'Everyone had a personal letter, hand-written in their pigeonholes, about how the season had gone for them, what they can do and how we're going to move forward as a club, et cetera. And I think that's his character. He was like a father figure in the dressing-room as well. He's the one who backed me and gave me that encouragement and support.'

And Langer's encouragement did not just come off the field. He was not shy in letting people know his feelings during a match. Suppiah remembers what it was like when the captain, batting at No.3, joined him in the middle: 'He would come down the wicket and tell you, "Come on, you've got to do this, you've got to switch on. Why have you played and missed?" He was at your face all the time, trying to get you to be disciplined.'

Langer got the best out of the squad and established Somerset as one of the finest teams in England. But it was not all his doing. Others played a huge role in their revival, including Rose. A Somerset legend having led them to their first major honour in 1979, Rose knew exactly what the good times at Taunton were like. And when he was appointed director of cricket in 2005, with the side languishing in Division Two, he was tasked with rebuilding the team. He did this by taking advantage of the Kolpak ruling, which allowed Somerset to sign three quality cricketers from South Africa without them being classed as overseas players.

The first to sign was Charl Willoughby. Having made two Test and three ODI appearances, the left-arm seamer joined them in 2006 once his international career had finished. 'I was playing at Leicester,' recalled Willoughby. 'The first game I played against Somerset was a TV game in the Cheltenham & Gloucester Trophy in 2005. I got 6-16 and Brian Rose took notice. A few weeks later they had signed Graeme Smith as their captain. Graeme and I were close friends at the time and the first game he played for them I got him out. And suddenly Rosey was like, "Who is this kid?" And Graeme just said to him, "If you want someone to get you 50 wickets a year, sign him." So he offered me a three-year deal at the end of the season on a Kolpak deal. I was the first Kolpak to go to Somerset.'

It proved to be a great signing. Willoughby picked up 66 first-class wickets in his first season, 62 in his second, and 54 in both his third and fourth. He was one of the most consistent bowlers in county cricket. Willoughby was joined at the County Ground two years later by Alfonso Thomas. The right-arm seamer, who played one Twenty20 for South Africa in 2007, was another excellent signing. He took 65 first-class wickets in his first two seasons and was also a good Twenty20 player, later going on to play in the Indian Premier League, Australia's Big Bash League and the Bangladesh Premier League. And there was Zander de Bruyn, who had played three Tests for South Africa. He went on to score 997 first-class runs during 2008, his debut season.

If anyone is unsure of just how good Willoughby, Thomas and de Bruyn were, the fact they received international caps during a time when Smith, Jacques Kallis, Hashim Amla, AB de Villiers, Shaun Pollock, Makhaya Ntini, Dale Steyn and Morne Morkel were playing for South Africa tells you everything you need to know. Rose had done well to get these players on board. 'Brian Rose did a really good job of finding players who were probably unheard of, certainly in English county cricket, and were good performers in South Africa,' explained Adam Dibble, a seamer who was just making his way into the squad. 'Tommo and Charl, Zander de Bruyn as well. They were really solid players who dabbled with international cricket a little bit and they came over and did really well. Obviously they weren't overseas players, so they were able to stay for a prolonged period of time. There was a bit of a South African backbone.'

Rose had also developed the club's academy. Somerset chairman Giles Clarke, who later became ECB chairman, demanded an emphasis on youth on appointing Rose in 2005. 'We have the whole of the south-west of England to draw upon and the club recognises the first and second team coaches do not have the time to spend working on this,' said Clarke. To achieve this, Hurry was brought back to the County Ground as head coach in 2006. Hurry had initially joined the club's backroom staff in 2001 after spending time as a fitness instructor in the Royal Marines, which is why he is affectionately known as 'Sarge' by his colleagues. He was promoted to coach the second team after a few years but left to coach the United Arab Emirates in 2005. His importance in Somerset's revival cannot be understated. It was he who persuaded Langer to return in 2007, even though he was ready to retire. He knew he needed Langer – a man who shared his hard-working, disciplined and loyal attitude – to be their captain if they were to become successful.

'My first season as head coach was 2006,' explained Hurry. 'It was a great year for me to really absorb, take in and get insight on what the strengths and areas of development were for within the club. There were a number of areas. The first one was that we needed more competition for places. The players in the second team needed to make sure they were performing to put the players in the first team under pressure. If the players who were established in the first team could feel the young players in the second team putting in performances with the bat and ball, that would grow their standard of performances. And the second thing was we really needed strong leadership on the field – respected leadership. And to help drive all that forward, it was important we identified the right character. So we were lucky in 2006 that JL came across as our Twenty20 overseas player and played a couple of Championship games as well. It became evident to me that he was a really strong candidate for that.'

With Hurry leading the first team, Rose had more time to work with Jason Kerr, the academy director and second-team coach, to produce quality talent. The most notable was Craig Kieswetter, who had emerged as one of English cricket's brightest talents. He had established himself as Somerset's number one wicketkeeper by 2010 and had made his England ODI debut. There was also Jos Buttler, who scored 554 runs for his school, King's College in Taunton, in 2009. For this he was named *Wisden*'s Schools Cricketer of the Year in 2010, following in the footsteps of Yorkshire's Jonny Bairstow and Leicestershire's James Taylor. Their rise through the academy was proof the emphasis on youth was beginning to pay off, much to Rose's credit. 'Brian was instrumental in setting everything off,' claimed Steve Kirby, the former Yorkshire and Gloucestershire seamer who joined Somerset in 2011. 'He galvanised a strong side together over time. He created a fantastic academy that Jason Kerr was a huge part of. In fact, it was him that brought people like Jos Buttler, Jack Leach, Max Waller and Chris Jones through. And now you're looking at Tom Banton and all those people. They all came through that set-up.'

Rose, Hurry and Langer had all done a great job, but the latter's exit meant they needed a new captain. The obvious choice was Trescothick. The 34-year-old had enjoyed an excellent career. He had more than 200 international caps to his name, scoring 26 centuries, captaining the Test side on two occasions and playing a crucial role in their Ashes victory in 2005. He was still a world-class cricketer when his international retirement meant he became a Somerset regular again in 2007, proven by the abundance of runs he scored. He made more than 1,000 first-class runs that summer and repeated the feat in 2008 and 2009. The latter was the most prolific of his career, scoring eight centuries and 1,817 runs in first-class cricket. Trescothick's return to the first team on a full-time basis was vital to their progression. 'If you look at 2007, where things turned around quite a lot, I think there was a fairly obvious benefit of having Marcus back from England,' said Munday.

With Langer's replacement in place, Rose began recruiting for the season. As well as losing Langer, they were also without Andy Caddick. The former England seamer had been a crucial member of the squad for nearly two decades, picking up 875 first-class wickets at an average of 25.80. Only five bowlers have been more prolific for Somerset. But as one international bowler left, another one arrived. Former India international Murali Kartik, who had previously played for Middlesex and Lancashire, had agreed to become their new overseas player. 'It's a new challenge for a player like me who has been playing first-class cricket in England for the last five seasons,' said Kartik on signing. 'I know it is not an Old Trafford or Lord's wicket because I've played here before and it is a different challenge to me … Somerset have been vying for honours for the last two years and I think I probably add a new dimension to their attack.'

And Kartik was not the only man to make the move from Middlesex. Nick Compton, the grandson of the great Denis, had also joined Somerset before the 2010 campaign. He had enjoyed a breakthrough season in 2006, scoring six first-class centuries at an average of 49.96. But he remained a Division Two player and was itching to prove himself in the top flight. Rose was keen to take on the 26-year-old, believing he had what it took to fill Langer's batting shoes. 'Nick is a player we view as having the ability to bat in our top three and be with us for many years,' said Rose as the signing was announced.

And the chance to succeed the Australian appealed to Compton. 'Ironically I took over from him if you could say that – I don't think anyone could fill his shoes,' he said. 'I had a relationship with him in the years before that. He's very much a character that I'd admired, particularly his philosophy on cricket. But also the fact that he opened the batting and was determined and gritty. Everything he said really resonated with me. There was a very human aspect to him, which just made me feel very normal. I read his books and really identified with his Buddhist philosophy. That was an area of self-discovery that really helped me in terms of visualising and trying to create my own aura.'

Rose was also important in getting him to sign on the dotted line. 'Brian Rose was probably one of the better cricket thinkers I've come across,' added Compton. 'He inspired me and was a man that I wanted to play cricket for. When he asked me and suggested coming down to

Somerset, he was very clear in his thinking. He wanted me to bat at No.3; he wanted a player that could occupy the crease and hold things together in the understanding that he had a lot of stroke-players and guys who could push the game on. And that's what I did well, I felt it was a position that I was made for. When I met him properly for the first time and sat down with him, it took about five minutes before I was like, "Where do I sign?"

'There was his attention to detail in terms of the make-up of the team. He went through each player, "Marcus Trescothick has scored this many runs in the last two years, but he's going to become captain now because Langer is leaving, so I expect a 30 per cent drop off. That means I need to make up this many runs. So and so is going to bat here, he's going to bat here." I'd never had a conversation like that with any cricketing director or coach. It'd been fairly relaxed in terms of, you know, you just played. Good players will excel. There hadn't been anything besides that until then. So when I sat down with him, I just bought into his vision completely. For me, I was always searching for that. I never lacked the drive, passion and ambition, but I wanted someone to measure up to that and when I met Brian, I couldn't have found somebody whose ambitions ran in line with mine as much.'

But above all else, Compton wanted to join Somerset because of their quality. 'When you consider that Somerset were one of the best teams in the country, it was a bit of a no-brainer,' he admitted. 'It was a great opportunity for me to go from Division Two and challenge myself in Division One at a great club with some great players. The chance to play with the likes of Trescothick, Charl Willoughby, Alfonso Thomas, James Hildreth, Kieswetter – there was a fantastic line-up of players. And their philosophy on performance, which was underpinned by Justin Langer. Somerset are a small club; you can't get away from that. And I don't mean a small club to be disrespectful to their history and legacy, but because of their location. They're stuck down in the south-west. So to get the club to a level of performance was no mean feat. It meant that a lot of changes had to be brought about and that comes only through real leadership and drive. In Langer and Andy Hurry, you had two people who drove that kind of ambition.'

While at this point in his career, Compton was only a big name thanks to his illustrious grandfather, the fact that he believed Somerset were going places and they could match his lofty ambitions says everything you need to know about what they had become under Rose, Hurry and Langer. They were now a force in English cricket and had an abundance of talent, experience and desire. For the first time in a long time, they were a team that could realistically win the Championship and other trophies. Going into the 2010 season, anything was possible.

* * * * *

Somerset's first Championship game of the summer was against Yorkshire at Headingley, a team that had narrowly survived relegation in both 2008 and 2009. As such, the visitors were the favourites. But after winning the toss and electing to bat, they made a meal of their innings. Notwithstanding Trescothick's defiant 117, Suppiah, de Bruyn and new boy Compton all failed to reach double figures. A useful 45 from Trego dragged them up to 272, giving himself and the rest of the attack something to bowl at. Yet they struggled as Joe Sayers, Tim Bresnan,

Adil Rashid and Andrew Gale all passed 50, with the latter going on to score a century. Despite Trego finishing with four wickets, Yorkshire posted a domineering 419. It was a particularly tough innings for Willoughby. He had bowled more overs than anyone, 29, and conceded 105 runs for his two wickets. And it had started so well for him after dismissing Adam Lyth with just his second ball.

For many seamers, bowling that many overs would be exhausting. But Willoughby would put a shift in for Somerset week in, week out. How he managed to keep himself fit had a lot to do with his professional development in South Africa. 'I've never been the most athletic sort of character,' admitted Willoughby. 'Bowling 80 to 82 miles per hour is not as stressful as bowling 90 miles per hour, but my whole make-up was based on a consistent action, which was not very stressful on the body. When I came into the professional game at a team called Boland, we didn't have any net bowlers. So the bowlers were just sort of ingrained into bowling for hours in the heat. And eventually I got to a stage where I might not have been the most athletic in all the bleep tests and that sort of stuff, but I was bowling-fit. And as long as I was bowling, I got fitter. Some of the bowlers would say, "How come you're always loose in the morning?" But I was just always loose and they were always stiff. I was very fortunate.'

And Willoughby was not the only Somerset bowler who could keep going. Thomas was also very fit and consistently performed in all formats. 'Tommo was very similar to me,' added Willoughby. 'He was like a little rubber man, he just kept going. But he came out of the same sort of make-up where there were no net bowlers in South Africa and we just had to bowl and bowl and bowl. And ultimately, our bodies just got used to it. Playing with Caddy was very similar. He couldn't run very well, but he would just bowl. And he would tell the captain when he was tired.'

Their stamina was not all down to their backgrounds, however. They were able to keep fit thanks to the work of Somerset's backroom staff, particularly Darren Veness, who was head of strength and conditioning. 'We had these bowlers who were just constantly playing and never broke down,' continued Willoughby. 'Nowadays, if you look at the team-sheets, the bowlers snap quite often. I don't know whether that's an element of bowling fitness or gym fitness or over-working certain things – I'm not an expert on it – but I did have a lot of mutual respect with our fitness guy, Darren Veness. He knew that if I was bowling-fit, he didn't have to worry about me. And if he wanted to try things with me and I didn't respond well to what it was doing to my body, he would just say, "Okay, we're not doing that – you tell me what you need to do to keep you on the park." And he had a lot of influence on keeping the guys on the park with that mutual respect.'

Kirby also highlights Veness's influence. 'When I moved to them, it was a surprise to me that they were so professional,' he said. 'Almost on another level, really. The fitness of the side was just remarkable. I thought I was a relatively fit bloke at that point, but they took my fitness to a whole new level. And that really came from a bloke called Darren Veness and the head physio there, a guy called Ian Brewer. They were absolutely excellent.'

The reason why fitness was so important was because Somerset wanted their players to be physically capable of challenging in all formats. 'Sarge and I worked together previously from the 2001 to the 2004 season,' explained

Veness. 'By the time Sarge came back in 2006, both of us knew the club and the players very well. We knew what we had to do there. Somerset hasn't changed, it's a small club that has every intention of punching way above its weight. So, the logic with that was always, "How are we going to maximise everything?" And again, we always had aspirations of pulling off all three trophies. There was never a mindset of targeting white-ball cricket, as some clubs clearly did in that era. The rationale was, "Let's get to the point physically that it's actually a sustainable option." Because it's all very well saying, "We're looking to compete." But if you're not physically able to cope with one format, you can't look to dominate three. It becomes a pointless statement. And it becomes less believable with the more injuries you get.

'The one thing that we know about cricket is it's a hard game, a tough game, and it takes its toll on the body. The logic was if we could get the lads strong, explosive and fast – with a good cardio base as well – the one thing we could look to reduce is the soft-tissue injuries. If we could reduce soft-tissue injuries significantly, then we've got a much better chance of Sarge being able to pick the same team every Monday. If everyone were able, you're in with a sniff because team consistency – we all know, we've seen the stats, we've seen the science behind it – would be one of the factors in doing well. A big factor was not having too many England selections, as well. Where I am now, at Surrey, we see lots of disruption through higher-level selection. We completely controlled the environment because there were no externals dipping in and picking our best players at the time.'

Despite Willoughby's frustration against Yorkshire, Somerset did fight back. Suppiah's 71 and de Bruyn's 83 allowed them to set a target of 198. But Lyth, who would go on to play for England, confirmed his class with a crucial 90 as Yorkshire reached their target with six wickets in hand. Somerset's season had started with a defeat, but they did not have time to sulk with a trip to Trent Bridge just around the corner. Nottinghamshire were one of the favourites for the title, having finished second for two consecutive years. And the visitors soon found out why after being sent in to bat. They slipped to 78/5 before Trego rescued the innings with a half-century. Knocks of 40-odd from Compton, Thomas and Damien Wright, an Australian all-rounder who had previously spent time at Northamptonshire, Glamorgan and Sussex, also helped as they posted a score of 272.

Wright and Thomas then started Somerset's revival with the ball. They took two wickets each and Willoughby claimed a four-for as he again bowled the most overs. Nottinghamshire were dismissed for 250 to give the visitors a slight advantage heading into the second innings. But they could not make it count as Stuart Broad proved irresistible. The England seamer picked up a five-for as Hildreth, de Bruyn and Kieswetter all failed to score. To make matters worse, Broad was not even supposed to be playing. He had asked to play as Nottinghamshire's other centrally contracted players, Graeme Swann and Ryan Sidebottom, missed out. 'Stuart feels that he needs a game and wants to play against Somerset,' said Nottinghamshire's director of cricket Mick Newell before the match. Broad, however, was no match for Trescothick. Aided by Wright's 78, he made 98 to get them from a worrying 43/6 to 216/8.

Somerset were eventually all out for 227, meaning the hosts had to repeat their first-innings score of 250 to win the match. And their chase started well. Bilal Shafayat made

49 and Mark Wagh 70. A collapse came as they had slipped from 127/2 to 198/6. But Amla, their star overseas player, was still at the crease. He remained unbeaten to guide Nottinghamshire to a two-wicket victory. It was a horrible start for Somerset, who had played two and lost two. They had not been hammered in either match, however, and it could have been a different story if Broad had chosen not to play. 'In fairness to that start, I was 12th man at a game at Trent Bridge where, effectively, Stuart Broad beat us in a spell,' remembered Munday.

Although it was only April, a crucial moment in the season had occurred. It would prove telling five months later. Yet Somerset could not think about that as they returned to Taunton. They were hosting Essex, the six-times Championship winners who had just been promoted from the second tier. And if they were going to beat them, they would have to do it without Kieswetter, who had been selected to play for England at the World Twenty20. As England went on to win the tournament – with Kieswetter being named player of the match in the final against Australia after scoring 63 – Somerset would be without their first-choice wicketkeeper until May. The man to fill his shoes was Buttler, who had made just one first-class appearance previously. Yet he was not fazed, scoring a rapid 36.

It was a joy for Phil Lewis to see Buttler succeed as a professional. Lewis is director of sport at King's College in Taunton, where Buttler spent his formative years. 'He was incredibly talented,' said Lewis. 'But that talent can only make 70 or 80 per cent of a player. The hard work that he put in made him the player he is. He was a real grafter; he loved spending time in the nets trying things out, always experimenting; he never stood back with what he was trying to learn and develop. Also, he's got all the shots, but I think people forget how good he is at the basics – things like his foot movement and how quick his hands work. That really set him apart from players of the same age as him.'

Half centuries from Compton, de Bruyn, Hildreth and Trego had got Somerset up to 387, putting them in control of the match. But a maiden first-class century from Billy Godleman allowed Essex to close the second day only five wickets down. Rain then descended upon Taunton, washing out the third day. 'We'll have a chat in the morning with Somerset captain Marcus Trescothick and see if we can set a game up,' said Essex coach Paul Grayson, hoping they could force a result. But the game faded into a draw. It was now three games without a win for Somerset, who faced a difficult trip to Old Trafford in their next match.

Lancashire were the Championship's form team having won two of their opening three matches. Yet it was the visitors who started well as Wright took three early wickets to reduce them to 27/3. And if it was not for Luke Sutton's century, Lancashire might have been in serious trouble. His 118, alongside Sajid Mahmood's 64, helped them post 292. After letting a strong position slip away, things got worse for Somerset as Suppiah and Compton fell cheaply. Thankfully for them, Trescothick's half-century steadied the ship before bad weather hit Old Trafford. Once the rain had disappeared on the third day, an excellent sixth-wicket partnership between Hildreth and Trego began. Trego scored a blistering ton off 83 balls and Hildreth, to the frustration of himself and statisticians everywhere, fell on 99. Nevertheless, they posted 383 and had something to bowl at. Lancashire, however, did not falter under pressure. They batted out the final day and Somerset remained winless. It was not the start to the season they had been hoping for.

* * * * *

Despite enduring a winless run in first-class cricket, Somerset got off to a flyer in the ECB 40 – county cricket's only one-day competition following the amalgamation of the One-Day Trophy, the 50-over competition, and the Pro 40 League. It was 40 overs per side, leaving England without a professional 50-over competition. They started their campaign with a comprehensive win against Glamorgan. A solid 73 from Compton and an unbeaten 68 from Hildreth helped them post a decent total of 224/5 before a quality bowling performance restricted Glamorgan to 186. In their next match against Lancashire, they posted a similar score of 235 when batting first, Suppiah top scoring with 80. And, as they had against Glamorgan, the attack bowled out their opponents for a below par score of 193. The star of the show was Thomas, who took four wickets to add to the three he picked up at Sophia Gardens.

Somerset then made it three wins from three against Unicorns, a new team, established during the previous winter to play specifically in the competition. On this occasion, Trescothick's team showed what they could do with the bat. With former Somerset all-rounder Keith Parsons, who appeared in 114 Championship matches for them between 1993 and 2006, scoring 53 to help Unicorns post 233, they required a solid effort from their top order. An unbeaten century from de Bruyn followed as they chased down their target within 37 overs. After a tough start to their Championship campaign, Somerset's one-day results were a welcome relief.

*　*　*　*　*

Somerset were back on the road for the fifth Championship match of the summer, travelling to the Rose Bowl in Southampton to face Hampshire. Although they had enjoyed cup success in recent years, winning the One-Day Trophy in 2005 and 2009, Hampshire had failed to win the Championship since 1973. Like Somerset, they were looking to end a long wait for red-ball success. The match started well for the visitors. Willoughby again proved his worth as he dismissed Michael Carberry and Jimmy Adams early on to leave Hampshire 18/2. Somerset then began to strengthen their grip on the contest. Neil McKenzie's 48 helped Hampshire recover, but with them on 123/5, Trescothick's side remained firmly in control. The arrival of Sean Ervine, however, changed everything. He hit an unbeaten 237 to lead Hampshire to 512.

With a win all but impossible, Somerset began clawing back the deficit. And they would have been in serious trouble had it not been for two excellent innings. The first came from Hildreth, who made amends for falling one short of a ton against Lancashire with an excellent 106. He was quickly reaffirming his position as one of county cricket's best middle-order batters and impressing Compton, his new colleague, in the process. 'A player whose talent amazed me was Hildreth,' said Compton. 'I think he's probably the most talented cricketer I've played with, along with Ian Bell. I just found him to be a very gifted individual. And I think even looking at the little subtleties – the way he fields or the way he catches – it was incredibly natural.'

Another supremely talented individual was Buttler, who scored his maiden first-class century to show why he was so highly rated at Taunton. His 144 helped Somerset secure a draw, a timely innings as Kieswetter was due to return home from the Caribbean with the World Twenty20 trophy just a few days later. With Kieswetter being the undisputed first-choice wicketkeeper at Somerset, Buttler's innings had proven that he could be trusted as a specialist batsman. It was the start of what Munday described as 'his breakthrough year'. Although he and Hildreth both had a reason to be cheerful, Trescothick did not. It was now five Championship games without a win. Their title hopes were dwindling.

Somerset's next match was against Yorkshire, the side who beat them in their opening fixture. If they wanted to make an impact on the title race, they needed to start winning. But it was Yorkshire that made a good start at the County Ground. Lyth scored a career-best 142 to help the visitors post 405. It was not all bad news for Somerset. Kartik's time in the Indian Premier League with Kolkata Knight Riders had come to an end and he was now available for selection. He marked his arrival at Taunton with three wickets. It was also a good innings for experienced seamer Ben Phillips, who had joined Somerset in 2007 after spending several seasons at Kent and Northamptonshire. The 35-year-old claimed four wickets to prove he was more than just a squad player.

Somerset's response started well. By the end of the third day, they were 226/4 with Suppiah well set on 78 not out. Unfortunately for him he was dismissed on 99 the next morning. Buttler, Suppiah's overnight partner, made 52 and a bit of wagging from the tail got them up to 377. They were back in the match, but not for long. Yorkshire ended the third day in control again as Lyth, a man Trescothick was glad to see the back of, made 93. The visitors continued to increase their lead the following morning as Anthony McGrath hit 83, before declaring on 333/4. Yorkshire had set Somerset 362 to win. With only 68 overs left to play, it was a tough – but gettable – target. And their chase started well. Trescothick made 53 and Compton hit 65.

The hosts needed to be more attacking, however. Coming in at No.4, de Bruyn picked up the tempo with 93 off 103 deliveries. But it was not until he was joined at the crease by Hildreth that things really got going. Hildreth, later aided by an unbeaten 31 from Buttler, hit an unbeaten 102 off just 70 balls to lead Somerset to their first win of the season. They did it with just 32 balls to spare. 'I scored a couple of hundreds last year, but this year I was looking for more consistency and trying to develop that through a more positive mindset,' said Hildreth after the match. 'It's brilliant batting with Jos as he scores freely and he's quite an attacking player. He doesn't build any pressure up for me at the other end. We had to pick our shots carefully and we got a lot of runs just by running hard between the wickets and picking up a few boundaries through the gaps.'

Somerset's victory against Yorkshire was a massive result – and just what they needed to kick-start their campaign. Next up was the visit of Warwickshire. After winning the toss and electing to field, an onslaught came from Somerset's attack. Thomas, taking a five-for, was the standout performer as the visitors were skittled out for 127. Warwickshire did reply with a few wickets before the end of the first day, but with Suppiah and Hildreth unbeaten on 61 and 35 respectively, the hosts were firmly in control.

Warwickshire responded well on the second day. Phillips, Kartik and Willoughby were all dismissed without scoring and if it had not been for another Hildreth century, the visitors would have been right back in the game. Hildreth's knock helped Somerset post 290 and take a lead of 163 into the second innings.

If Warwickshire were going to give themselves a chance, they needed to score big at the second attempt. But Kartik was simply irresistible on the spinning Taunton deck, taking six wickets as they were dismissed for 207. The result was a formality from there and Somerset knocked off the 40-odd runs required with nine wickets in hand to make it two wins on the bounce. Nine days later, they travelled to Edgbaston for the return. It was the team's last Championship match until 20 July, a gap of nearly seven weeks. With such a break, it was important they made it three wins from three if they wished to keep their good red-ball form going. On this occasion, they were batting first and managed to post a steady score of 268. Half-centuries from Trescothick and Hildreth, who was quickly becoming the team's standout performer, put them in a solid position.

It is an innings fondly remembered by Suppiah, but not for the reasons you may think. 'I got out around five minutes before lunch and I only managed two runs,' he remembered. 'It was funny and sort of unreal because I just couldn't lay a bat on anything! The wicket was very difficult and dry and the seamers were not particularly easy to play because it was an up-and-down wicket. I just stuck in; played and missed quite a few; got struck on the head, I remember Boyd Rankin hitting me. You would have thought you'd have nicked one past slip for four, but it just didn't happen and I just got stuck on two runs for

nearly two hours. Tres was there on 40-odd before lunch.
And I remember getting out five minutes before lunch. I
came back into the dressing-room and just started laughing,
everyone burst out laughing … The moral of the story is
that the partnership was vital because I'd done my job for
the lower order to come in and get their runs. I'd tired out
the bowlers and the new ball.'

In reply, Warwickshire again struggled to handle Kartik
as he took five wickets to restrict them to 140. They did
fight back in the second innings, reducing Somerset to 183.
And their target would have been even smaller if it were not
for Phillips, who scored 55 to take the lead past 300. In the
end, Somerset did not need those runs as the hosts, with
Kartik picking up another six wickets, were bowled out for
130. The spinner's efforts had ensured a third consecutive
victory for Somerset and they were now up to third in the
table. Compton already knew how good Kartik was having
played with him at Middlesex, describing him as 'the best
left-arm spinner I've played with'. Now his new team-mates
were also beginning to appreciate his value. 'He's a very,
very good spinner,' said Suppiah. 'His knowledge of cricket
was very good. He would come up and suggest things and
all that. It would give us a different perspective of cricket.'

One player who benefited from Kartik's time at Somerset
was George Dockrell, a promising young slow left-armer.
He was able to spend time with Kartik in the nets and learn
more about the art of spin, enjoying priceless lessons that
helped him develop into a fine international cricketer for
Ireland. 'Murali Kartik was probably on his own level in
terms of the control he had,' admitted Dockrell. 'When I
spoke to him about what he would try and do during nets or
during games, the level he was working at was remarkable.

He'd talk me through a net, ball by ball, and exactly what he was going to do for every ball and exactly what the batter was going to do because he wanted them to do it. Shane Warne is one of the spinners they talk about when every single ball is part of a plan and I think Murali Kartik had that level of control, plus the skill and the game theory to actually do that. Getting to see him play and watching him do what he used to do was, for me, a highlight and I probably still haven't talked to another spinner like that since who operated at that level.'

Kartik's quality was helping Somerset recover from their difficult start to the season. He was the final piece in the puzzle. They had excellent batsmen in Suppiah, Trescothick, Hildreth and Compton, two quality wicketkeepers in Kieswetter and Buttler, two superb all-rounders in Trego and de Bruyn and great seamers in Willoughby and Thomas. And now they had a mesmerising spinner in Kartik. Although Langer had departed, Somerset were better than ever. One of the things that made them such a top side, in Suppiah's eyes, was that each player knew exactly what their job was. 'As individuals, we knew our roles, which gave us a lot of clarity,' he said. 'For example, if we were in a certain situation and we needed X amount of runs in so many overs, everyone knew who the man would be to do the job.'

Compton agrees. 'I could just feel that every player was focused, focused on doing their job and making sure they played their role,' he added. 'And it was just a great atmosphere and a great team to be a part of when you had such consistent professionals, guys at the top of their game. Alfonso Thomas was a serious wicket-taking bowler, Zander de Bruyn was a world-class all-rounder at times.

We had all bases covered and just a great team to be a part of. Everyone was kind of at the peak of their performance. I don't think any of them were going to get much better, apart from myself, Hildreth, Kieswetter and Buttler, those who were slightly younger. With every good team, you need a core group of senior players. To have the experience and durability of Zander de Bruyn, Alfonso Thomas, Charl Willoughby, Marcus Trescothick – you're not going to get many better senior players than that.'

Willoughby also believes the team's strong core was their greatest strength. 'The key was the fact we had a lot of very experienced players and some young, up-and-coming players like Craig Kieswetter, Jos Buttler and Lewis Gregory,' he said. 'The core of our side was made up of very well-established cricketers such as Langer, Trescothick, Hildreth, Peter Trego, Zander de Bruyn, Nick Compton, me and Alfonso Thomas. You had a lot of cricketers who knew their game inside out. They were able to handle pressure situations through their experience as well as their ability. It gave us that sort of real fight within the team. Any situation we got ourselves into, we knew how to get out of.'

For Hurry, much of their success was down to young players breaking into the first team and challenging the likes of Willoughby for their shirt. 'Let's not forget Marcus came out of international cricket and he became available for us,' said Hurry. 'That made a big difference. We had a great combination of some experienced players and some very high-potential young players coming through: Hildreth, Kieswetter, [Neil] Edwards, Suppiah. If you dovetail that in with Langer, Trescothick, Caddick, Willoughby ... We also made a couple of key signings. We got Peter Trego back to the club. We also identified and recruited Ben Phillips from Northants. Combine that, with some really hungry players in the second team, we had a really good formula to be really competitive.'

Yet all this would have been irrelevant if they had not maintained their hard-working attitude. 'We had the guys who were flair players – Kieswetter, Buttler, Trego – but we also had a lot of consistent players, guys who just did their job and did not get much glory for what they did,' added Willoughby. 'Zander de Bruyn; Compo to a degree. People like me, who just chipped away with wickets all the time. Murali Kartik, who was a bit of a flair player, but would also guarantee you 50 wickets. Peter Trego, who never got much credit for what he did. Even though he was a flair player, he would literally turn up every single game in every single format and put in the hard yards.'

Dibble shares Willoughby's view. 'The approach was a lot different to what it had been previously,' he said. 'The whole professional and international influence that Langer brought. And having Tres for the whole time after he'd finished with England, obviously he was still good enough to play for England. There was that core – an international heartbeat. And then there were these guys who had dabbled with international cricket from South Africa. Having those players in their mid-30s, with a lot of experience and being high-performing players, buying into what Langer brought in terms of being professional and hard-working. Langer and Andy Hurry got on really well because they are very similar people, in terms of fighting hard and team spirit.'

Somerset were now the finished article. They were one of the best teams in England; perhaps the best considering how they competed in all formats. Even in the days of Garner, Botham and Richards, they were not as strong as this in first-class cricket. When they were promoted in 2007, honours had become a possibility again. Now, they were a probability. Never had they had a better chance to win their maiden Championship title.

* * * * *

Before their Twenty20 campaign began, Somerset had two 40-over matches to play. The first was against Sussex, a game remembered for another wonderful Hildreth innings. Having been reduced to 109/4 in pursuit of 292, their chances looked slim. But then came Hildreth's knock. With the help of an excellent half-century from Buttler, he hit an unbeaten 100 off just 66 deliveries to lead them to victory with nine balls remaining. In their next match against Worcestershire at Bath, however, Hildreth was dismissed for a second-ball duck as Somerset set their guests 235 to win. Half-centuries from Kieswetter, de Bruyn and Phillips did the business for them on this occasion. In response Worcestershire struggled with the right-arm pace of Mark Turner. The 25-year-old, who joined Somerset from Durham in 2006, picked up career-best one-day figures of 4-36 as Worcestershire were dismissed for 164. The result made it five wins from five for Somerset.

Then came the start of the Twenty20 Cup. The competition, which began in 2003 as a replacement for the Benson and Hedges Cup, was quickly becoming the pinnacle of the English summer as demand for Twenty20 cricket grew. Somerset's opening fixture was a horrible away tie to Sussex, where they were dismissed for 103 after the hosts had scored 155/7. Kieswetter top scored with 47. They were set a target of 156 in their next match against Middlesex at Lord's, but they had no trouble with the bat on this occasion. West Indies international Kieron Pollard, a white-ball specialist signed exclusively to play in the tournament, hit a 45-ball 89 to see them home with more than two overs to spare.

Pollard went on to finish the tournament with 354 runs, struck at a rate of 175.24. He also dismissed 29 batsmen at an average of 15.10, a tally bettered by only two players. 'Kieron showed himself to be the sort of player who can change a game in a very short period of time,' said Rose on signing him. Although Pollard did well, Thomas, the leading wicket-taker in the tournament with 33, was Somerset's best Twenty20 player. For Compton, what made him such an excellent performer across all formats was his character. 'Alfonso Thomas's competitiveness was something that shone out,' claimed Compton. 'If I look at key players and players who carried the competitiveness and backbone of that team, it was players like Alfonso with his personality.'

Yet it was not just sheer desire that made Thomas special. He conceded just 6.31 runs per over during that season's Twenty20 Cup. In comparison to others who bowled a minimum of 300 deliveries, only Glamorgan's Robert Croft was more economical at 5.93. 'He was probably one of the best death bowlers in the country at that point, if not the best,' said Kirby. 'It was great to have an opportunity to learn from him. He was always really helpful to me.'

When Kirby arrived at Somerset, he was immediately struck by the quality of the white-ball team. 'They were a fantastic group of players and a fantastic group to be involved with,' explained Kirby. 'We had all bases covered. It was such a dangerous side with our top four, top five batting line-up. We had Trescothick, Kieswetter, Pollard,

Hildreth. And then obviously coming in at No.6 was Jos Buttler! So very rarely did we bat past that point. When we played a Twenty20 game, it was always either Pollard or Buttler going in around the 11th over. At Taunton we were always very dangerous in the powerplay, blasting people all over the place. It wasn't a good place to come and bowl, I can tell you that! Bowlers got quite scared really. You could see they didn't know where to bowl on a flat pitch against such a devastating batting line-up. We were smashing 190s, 200s out regularly.'

Somerset's win against Middlesex kick-started their Twenty20 campaign. They went on to win 11 of their 16 matches to finish top of the table and qualify for the quarter-finals. Only Warwickshire secured as many victories during the group stage. And there were some big performances during that time. Kent were bowled out for 105, Trescothick scored a 27-ball 78 against Hampshire and they hit 204 against Middlesex at Taunton. Having reached the final in 2009, Somerset were well on their way to getting there again.

* * * * *

Somerset returned to Championship action in late July. They started well against Kent at Taunton, reaching 101/1. But then came a dramatic collapse as they slipped to 118/7. They were only saved when rain halted play shortly after the seventh wicket fell. Despite collapsing, Somerset did fight back. They clawed their way to 205 and then dismissed Kent for 172, with Kartik taking another five-for. But just as things were looking up, the rain returned. There was no play on the third day and by the time the hosts declared on 301/7, they had little more than two sessions left to bowl Kent out. And it was not long enough as they resisted Somerset's attack. Although Kartik finished with ten wickets in the match, they came up three wickets short as former England wicketkeeper Geraint Jones survived 150 deliveries. It may not have been a defeat, but it was a blow to Somerset's title hopes.

Their next opponents were Nottinghamshire at the County Ground, who were right in the mix for the title having won four consecutive matches at the start of the season. Despite Trescothick being bowled first ball of the match by Darren Pattinson, they posted 517 thanks to another Hildreth century and fifties from Buttler, Kieswetter and Trego. In response, the visitors reached 339 before Willoughby finished the innings with a six-for. That was not enough to avoid the follow-on and Nottinghamshire were made to bat again, labouring to 190. This time it was Thomas who took the spoils, picking up a five-for to all but win the match. Trescothick and Compton knocked off the 13 needed with ease. Somerset were back to winning ways in emphatic fashion.

After two home games, Somerset were back on the road for a trip to Canterbury. The first day was another run-fest as Suppiah and Hildreth both scored centuries to help them reach 363/7. They shared an important partnership as the visitors had slipped to 59/3, one which brought back many happy memories for Suppiah. He grew up batting alongside Hildreth at Millfield, an independent school in the heart of Somerset. The school was founded by first-class cricketer Jack Meyer in the 1930s and has since established a reputation for developing talented cricketers such as Kieswetter and Simon Jones, a member of England's 2005 Ashes-winning squad. 'We went through a difficult period, but Hildy and I managed to put a partnership together and brought back some school-day memories, which was great,' recalled Suppiah.

Somerset were dismissed for 380 the next morning before Kent, aided by a rain-affected second day, hit 372 to take the game away from them. And it was Geraint Jones who made the difference again, hitting 178 to frustrate Somerset's attack. 'Towards the end of my innings I felt at ease and still and almost able to hit the ball where I wanted,' said Jones at the end of the third day, knowing he had all but secured a draw. As victory was no longer an option, Trescothick decided to take his frustration out on Kent's attack during the final day. He smashed an unbeaten 188 as Rob Key, Kent's skipper, dismissed Trego and Phillips. Key would finish his career in 2015 with just three first-class wickets to his name.

Hampshire were Somerset's next opponents at Taunton. After winning the toss and deciding to field, rain and England batsman Michael Carberry frustrated them. He scored 71 as rain washed out most of the first two days. The hosts did not get a chance to bat until the end of the second day, when Hildreth hammered another century. He was eventually dismissed for 130 as Somerset, knowing victory was no longer possible, were dismissed for 412. Hampshire went on to score 224/4 before the match finished as a draw. 'There just was not enough time left in the game,' said Trescothick, who could take solace in Somerset's position in the table. They were now second in the Championship, having gone ten matches unbeaten. Heading into the business end of the season, they were in with a chance of winning all three trophies. Everything was to play for …

* * * * *

Before their next Championship match, Somerset travelled to the Rose Bowl for Twenty20 Finals Day alongside Nottinghamshire, Hampshire and Essex. Since the competition's inception in 2003, the semi-finals and final have always been played at the same ground on the same day, giving fans the chance to enjoy a festival of Twenty20 cricket. Somerset had reached the last four after hammering Northamptonshire at Taunton. They had surpassed Northamptonshire's below-par total of 112/6 in 17 overs. Most of the squad already knew what Finals Day was all about having lost to Sussex 12 months previously. But for Pollard, it was a whole new experience – and one he could not wait for. 'Saturday will be one of the biggest games for me, getting the opportunity to play a final in the county arena,' said Pollard, aged 23 at the time. 'Hopefully we can go there and go one step further.'

Yet he was wary of their opponents. Nottinghamshire had arguably the best Twenty20 bowling attack in the country as Sidebottom, Swann and Broad were part of the England team that conceded fewer than 150 runs in each match during their victorious World Twenty20 campaign three months earlier. They also had Samit Patel, who finished the Twenty20 Cup with an excellent economy rate of 6.50, and Dirk Nannes, a key member of Australia's Twenty20 attack. But Pollard, a confident young man, was up for the challenge. 'They have a very good bowling attack,' he said. 'A lot of their guys have played for England. The five of them are top-class bowlers. It'll be a tough challenge for us, but I think we're up for that challenge. You can play for England, for the West Indies or for South Africa but you've still got to go out there and put bat on ball.'

After winning the toss, Nottinghamshire captain David Hussey, a member of the Australia side that lost to England in the World Twenty20 Final, decided to put their attack to good use and send Somerset in to bat. Yet it proved to be a poor decision. Trescothick carried on his good form by hitting 60, Pollard made an unbeaten 23 and Buttler hit 55 to post a very good score of 182/5. Considering the quality of Nottinghamshire's attack, it was an innings that demonstrated just how good Somerset were. In response, their opponents struggled. Swann, opening the batting, made only 11, as did Alex Hales, coming in at No.3. But then they started scoring at a rate of knots. Patel hit 39 off 26 balls and Hussey made an unbeaten 27 before rain intervened. The Duckworth/Lewis method judged Somerset to be the winners by a mere three runs. They had scraped through.

In the final they faced Hampshire, who had narrowly beaten Essex at the beginning of the day. Trescothick's side would have been confident of finishing the job after beating them home and away during the group stage. Kieswetter led the charge with 71 off 59 balls. His efforts, along with a quickfire 22 from Pollard, helped them post a good score of 173/6. It had come at a cost, however. Pollard was forced to retire after he was struck on the helmet by a bouncer. Not only had Somerset missed his power towards the end of their innings, but he was unable to bowl in the final. It was a huge loss. Their attack was now a man down and they struggled to stop the flow of runs as McKenzie made a half-century to keep Hampshire in the match.

In the end, it went down to the final ball. Hampshire, on 172/5, needed a single to win by virtue of having lost fewer wickets. Dan Christian, the man on strike, had pulled his hamstring and had Adams running for him at square leg, just to add to the chaos. As de Bruyn delivered the all-important ball, it crashed into Christian's pads and skewed away. It looked as if it was hitting leg stump, but the umpire disagreed and during the appeal, the field froze as Christian limped through for a single. Confusion ensued, but Trescothick soon realised they had lost. 'I've never seen a last over like that,' said the winning skipper Dominic Cork. 'It had everything – changes of ball, runners, wickets, the lot. It was a chaotic last two overs but I'm proud of all the guys for taking us over that winning line.'

It was, and remains, the most dramatic conclusion to a Twenty20 match in English domestic history – and an important moment in the history of the format. Twenty20 cricket is often described by those who dislike it as forgettable. Some claim that because of its duration, it fails to leave a lasting impression. Yet the 2010 Twenty20 Cup Final was one of the first to disprove that theory. Although they were losers, this Somerset team had become part of cricketing history. A man that was due to sign for them shortly after the final was Kirby, who was at the Rose Bowl to witness the dramatic conclusion. 'Looking back on it, I didn't even know what the rules were with the runner and all,' he recalled. 'It was one of those difficult things to watch.'

While it may have been hard for Kirby, it was much more difficult for Michael Bates, Hampshire's wicketkeeper, to endure. 'It was an amazing game,' remembered Bates. 'We were all so young. In our Hampshire team we had a handful of pretty experienced players, but we also had a handful of us young lads who were about 19, 20 years old and had grown up playing together. To be honest, looking back on it, it was all just a massive blur. With all the confusion at the end as well, no one was quite sure whether we'd won it. I know the Somerset lads were in a huge confusion out in the middle as to what to do. You had Dan Christian limping around at the non-striker's end having wrongly taken a single when he should have just stood there. And I think when it all boiled down to it, with hindsight, had one of the Somerset players taken the bails off to effectively run Dan Christian out then we would have lost.'

As Bates and his team-mates rejoiced, Somerset sobbed. The controversy had not gone in their favour and they had suffered heartbreak in Hampshire. It is a match that still haunts Trescothick. In an interview in 2018 he said, 'There was suddenly this presence, this air of, "The game is not finished? What's going on? What have I missed?" ... The umpire came to me at the end and said, "You do realise that if you would have thrown the ball in and taken the stumps out and appealed, you would have won the game?" Then that horrible, sinking feeling comes in and you walk off thinking, "Oh my God, we've just thrown it away." And that was it, done and dusted. We're eight years on ... and it still lives with me to this day.'

And that is no surprise considering how unlucky Somerset were. History remembers the confusion at the end, but if Pollard had not been injured, he would have probably added more runs and made an impact with the ball. That could have made it a comfortable victory. And there was the lbw appeal at the end. In fairness to the umpire, it was a very close call and could have been missing leg stump. The benefit of the doubt must be given to the batsman, especially with the Decision Review System not in use. Yet that decision could have so easily gone the other way. Ultimately, Somerset just had to accept that it was not meant to be their day. Their season was still very much alive, however, as they had a realistic chance of winning both the Championship and the one-day tournament. They could not grieve about their loss. They had to pick themselves up and go again.

* * * * *

Just days after Finals Day, Somerset travelled to Essex to get their season back on track. The Championship match was held at Castle Park in Colchester, a ground no longer used for first-class cricket. After winning the toss, Trescothick endured a nightmare start, dismissed by David Masters for a third-ball duck, which set the tone for the innings. The visitors failed to build on good starts and if it were not for Hildreth's 84, they would have been in real trouble. They were bowled out for 215. Thanks to their attack, though, they were able to take a lead into the second innings. Willoughby and Thomas took four wickets each as Essex were dismissed for 151. Then came an onslaught from Trescothick. He hit an unbeaten 228 off just 230 deliveries before declaring with the score on 367/8. It was a very impressive innings, especially when you consider that Suppiah, Kieswetter, Phillips and Thomas were all sent back to the shed without scoring.

With Somerset in such a dominant position and the sun shining bright, the result was a formality. Essex were dismissed for 212, with de Bruyn taking four wickets, to complete a 219-run victory. Trescothick then continued his impressive form in the next match as champions Durham visited Taunton. Batting first, he and Suppiah put on 119 for the first wicket. It was one of many great partnerships shared between the two during Suppiah's time at the top of the order. 'I was pretty much sandwiched between two cricket greats in Trescothick and Langer at three,' laughed Suppiah. 'Opening with Tres was amazing. I still remember our partnerships over the five years.

'We actually had a lot of things in common, not in terms of how we played – obviously he was easier on the eye and had more talent – but in terms of watching the ball, what the bowlers were trying to do. We worked as a partnership in that sense. So while I was at the non-striker's end, I would look out for where the shine was and how the bowler was holding it. I would then convey that message and vice versa. We were very much into that, being very detailed. When we were playing, he would just play his game and I would play my game. There were days when Tres would be on 100 and I was still stuck on 20. But that was fine; that was the partnership; that was what was important. Sometimes I would be ahead of him. We worked as a partnership really well.'

When Suppiah departed for 54, Compton joined Trescothick in the middle and the duo built another big partnership, worth 113 runs. As someone who wanted to play international cricket, it was a joy for Compton to learn from his esteemed colleague. 'Trescothick was a serious player,' said Compton. 'Marcus wasn't a man of many words, if I'm to be honest, in terms of helping me with my batting. And I don't mean that he wasn't a help. But I think he helped more by the way he went about his own game. Out of the side of your eye, it was hard not to watch him and how he conducted himself … There was kind of a culture that you couldn't help but follow. Being a top-order player, most of my batting was done with Trescothick. I think we scored quite a lot of runs together. There was just a maturity and a way that he went about things that had a huge impact on me. And it was probably only in the years afterwards when I realised how much he rubbed off on me.'

It was a pleasant return to the side for Compton, who made 45 before departing. He had endured a tricky start to his Somerset career, making just one Championship appearance between late May and late August. He had been dropped during the home match against Warwickshire having made just four in the first innings. With Suppiah, Trescothick, de Bruyn, Hildreth and Kieswetter all established in the team, Somerset were forced to choose between Compton and Buttler. Unfortunately for Compton, they chose the latter. 'I was very lucky when I came that I hit it at their top point,' said Compton, remembering his first season at Somerset. 'Langer had been there for the three years before that, made a lot of changes and I hit the up-curve of that. I had some success at Middlesex and had been on an England A tour. And that year, 2009, I actually had a great year in all forms of the game. I averaged 72 in one-day cricket, which wasn't something I was particularly associated with. I also had a pretty good year in Championship cricket – I scored nearly 900 runs.

'When I arrived, I remember being quite overwhelmed by the level of professionalism and performance as well as the talent and expertise in the group. I'd probably not been at that level before, notwithstanding Middlesex had some outstanding players. I played in a couple of very good teams. When I came to Somerset, it was a real jump in terms of attitude and expectation. There was an expectation that we would win. Going into the first few games, there was less hope and more of, "How are we going to win this game?"

And if we didn't win that game, it was almost an anomaly. Something had gone wrong, but it would go right in the next game. You almost jumped up 50 per cent in terms of the belief walking on to the field, "This is what we expect from us as a group." If you didn't fit into that or live up to that, you were out of the team.

'When I first arrived, I wouldn't say I was intimidated. I was very keen to impress and to be successful. And the way I tried to go about was to try and impress those players around me by my stroke-play, which I knew I had. But I think when I went towards that I became less consistent. I got a couple of scores here and there, but I was only averaging late 20s and not really fulfilling the role they wanted. And I think Jos Buttler scored a hundred at No.6 and they put him in at No.3 and dropped me for a few games. That was after being at the club for around three months. And, of course, the change in culture was very different. You can imagine being in London to coming down to Somerset. I would say I felt a little bit alone down there. It's a place that's quiet, parochial and people do stick to themselves. So the first three months I was kind of in a flat, in the middle of Taunton and trying to find my feet. So I found that, initially, quite difficult.'

The turning point in Compton's Somerset career was a conversation he had with Rose during his stint in the second team. 'Brian Rose came up to me,' he recalled. 'He wasn't a man of many words. He had a cricketing experience that you respected. He had a look in his eye that you knew he meant business. Obviously, I wasn't as happy as I should've been and he just said, "I got you down here to bat and bat all day. Just don't get out." I went out there in that second-team game and I remember just feeling like it was easy.

There was only one thought in my mind, "Don't get out." If the ball was outside off stump, I left it; if it was straight, I defended it; if it was on my legs, I probably got some runs; if it was a poor ball, I hit it. I just wasn't getting out – and I did that for hours. I ended up with a hundred in a second-team game and it wasn't anything special. But I'd got a hundred. And I think I scored three hundreds in a row for the second team and got back into the first team, averaging 45 for the remaining games in 2010.

'That was very much the becoming of the player I became. There were strokes there, there were hundreds and I could hit the ball. But the message I got was just so clear. And whenever things got a little bit cloudy, I just thought, "I'm not going to get out." I knew that Hildreth and Kieswetter and all these guys, if I could stay there at the crease, the team was just going to be a much better team. I broke the game down and made it very simple. If I'm there at the crease, then we're not going to get bowled out before the end of the day. And if we don't get bowled out before the end of the day – with this batting line-up – we'll have a score that's competitive. But if I get out early, then there might be vulnerability in our team. So it was a very simple logic for me. I just batted. Even if I got nought off 100 balls, the team was still doing very well. And I just grew in confidence, in terms of my role and the specifics of what I did.'

Compton had not just turned a corner in his Somerset career, but in his professional career. He had overcome a dark time in his cricketing life and there were some great times on the way. But first, he had to help Somerset beat Durham. Trescothick's innings eventually came to an end on 128 as they reached 287/4. They were in a solid position, but then rain intervened. The second and third days were washed out leaving Somerset to bat on in a bid to gain as many bonus points as possible. They declared on 400/6 before Durham openers Michael Di Venuto and Mark Stoneman saw out the final 15 overs. The result had hampered Somerset's title bid, leaving them 16 points adrift of leaders Nottinghamshire having played a game more. They could not worry about their rivals, however, as they had a home fixture against Lancashire to focus on.

The match at Taunton started well, with Willoughby taking four wickets to restrict Lancashire to 259. Somerset were frustrated by rain, losing much of the second day, but they still managed to build a big lead. When their innings came to an end during the third morning, they had scored 382 as Kieswetter, Trego and Kartik all made half-centuries. At this point, their title bid hung in the balance. Although they had a lead of 123, time was not on their side. But showing fighting spirit, they dismissed Lancashire for 170. They then pushed to get the game finished. With an unbeaten 26 from Compton they knocked off the 48 runs required and, with Nottinghamshire losing consecutive matches against Durham and Yorkshire, Somerset were just two points behind the leaders heading into the final match of the season. It was all to play for.

The Championship title was not the only thing up for grabs. Despite losing the Twenty20 Final, Somerset were still going well in the ECB 40. Before the Twenty20 break, they had won five out of five in the tournament. And they picked up where they left off when play resumed in late July. A huge 94-run win over Surrey at the Oval was followed up with convincing victories against Unicorns and Lancashire, making it eight straight wins in one-day cricket. Although they suffered defeats to Sussex and Worcestershire, their imperious form continued. They inflicted a mammoth defeat on Glamorgan at Taunton, hitting 368/4 – with Trego scoring 147 and Buttler, at his destructive best, hitting an unbeaten 90 off just 33 balls – before bowling them out for 119.

Somerset's reward for finishing top of their group was a home semi-final against Essex. Unsurprisingly, it was another brutal display from the hosts. There were half-centuries from Trescothick and Compton as they posted 312/6. Essex, forced to play aggressively, consistently lost wickets as they sought to chase down the big target. Kartik picked up two of those wickets as he conceded just 40 runs from his eight overs. In the end Essex were bowled out for 217 inside 30 overs, completing a 95-run victory for Somerset. 'I thought Somerset played exceptionally well,' admitted Essex captain James Foster after the match. 'I definitely think they're the benchmark in all forms of the game at the moment.'

Somerset were heading to Lord's, but not before the Championship finale against Durham at Chester-le-Street. Sitting in second place behind Nottinghamshire, they needed to defeat the defending champions and hope results elsewhere went their way. The odds were against them, but they had never had a better chance to win the Championship. Quite simply, it was the biggest first-class match in the club's history. They did not get the start they required, however. The match did not begin until after 3pm because of rain and when it did, Dale Benkenstein frustrated them. Durham's No.4 made an unbeaten 71 as they closed on 132/2. 'He's a really fine player and he played very well,' said a frustrated Rose. 'The first session on Tuesday morning will be vital. They've done very well to only lose two wickets, but there's still everything to play for.'

Yet Somerset were not the only team to suffer from the bad weather. Just six balls were bowled during the first day of Nottinghamshire's match against Lancashire at Old Trafford, giving Somerset the upper hand in the title race. And things got better for them during the next 24 hours. More rain descended upon Manchester as just 27 overs were possible during the second day. Meanwhile at Chester-le-Street, Somerset had quickly ended Durham's innings. They were dismissed for 286 with Phillips taking four wickets. The visitors then made quick runs. Trescothick scored 75 off just 89 deliveries as they closed on 226/4. After acquiring both bowling and batting points, Somerset were now above Nottinghamshire in the table. Everything seemed to be falling into place.

Both matches continued to go in Somerset's favour on the third day. No play was possible at Old Trafford, allowing Somerset to increase their advantage. A seventh Championship century of the summer from Hildreth and a brutal half-century from Trego helped them post 426 and take a lead of 140 into the second innings. Durham managed to claw that deficit back before the end of the day, reaching 171/2 at the close. Nevertheless, they had picked up four more batting points as Nottinghamshire remained in the pavilion. But the next morning Durham dug in. Michael Di Venuto scored 129, while Benkenstein and Gordon Muchall used up 199 precious deliveries between them. When their innings eventually ended, Somerset needed 181 inside 17 overs. They gave it their best shot, promoting Kieswetter, Buttler and Trego up the order, but they could only manage 48. The match finished in a draw and Somerset picked up just three more points.

So, to win the title, Nottinghamshire required nine points. And the morning went in their favour. Batting with blue skies above, they went about their business proficiently. Adam Voges scored a century and Patel made a blistering 96 off 91 balls. To have any chance of winning the title, they needed to reach 400 and achieve maximum batting points. And for a while, it looked like they would fall just short as they crawled to 390/9. Yet England bowlers Sidebottom and Pattinson got them over the line. They declared on 400/9 in a bid to get the three wickets they required to claim an all-important bowling point. But with them only having 16 overs, there was still a very good chance Somerset could be crowned champions. As they shook hands at Chester-le-Street, the team quickly made their way to the nearest television they could find to watch the drama unfold.

Somerset were powerless, however, to stop Sidebottom and Andre Adams. They dismissed Karl Brown, Mark Chilton and Shiv Chanderpaul within five overs – and just as the rain was starting to fall again. Nottinghamshire, having picked up 214 points, the same amount as Somerset, were declared champions by virtue of having won more matches. 'The vast majority just said let's go out and bash 400 and take three wickets,' said a delighted captain Chris Read after the match. 'Last night a lot of the guys got together and had a chat about what we should do. This morning we were devastated to see we weren't going to start on time because we thought it might scupper our plans. But we decided, on balance, the best route was to back ourselves to get 400. My dad is a lifelong Somerset fan so he will have mixed emotions, and I grew up in Devon watching

Somerset as a lad. For them to come so close to their first ever Championship, they must feel gutted, but they can take heart from probably being the form side of the summer in all forms of the game.'

While Read's sentiment would have been appreciated, it meant little as Somerset's dream was left in tatters. The class of 2010 had missed a golden opportunity to become the first team to bring the Championship trophy back to Taunton. 'The lads are pretty disappointed after a long, hard season and a lot of hard work put in to be second again,' said Trescothick after Nottinghamshire had clinched the all-important third wicket. 'It's gutting, really. It's terrible. Something that will live with us for a long, long time to know we were so close – touching distance to the trophy – but so far away when Notts got that third wicket. Any time you lose a big cup or a final it's disappointing. Twenty20 Finals Day still haunts me even though we're six weeks away from it, but with this being the elusive trophy for the club it is going to hurt, no doubt about it.'

And a decade later, it still hurts. 'The bitter side of it was the last game at Durham,' recalled Suppiah. 'I remember us finishing our game and we shook hands and the Notts and Lancashire match was on the telly. We all thought, "Okay, three wickets in X amount of overs, Lancashire can do this – especially with Chanderpaul in their line-up." And then we saw the first wicket go and it was like, "Oh, great." A few of the boys just stepped outside because they couldn't watch it anymore. And then the second wicket fell and I was like, "What the hell is going on here?" It was unreal. And eventually the third wicket fell and that was a bitter pill to swallow because we had one hand on the trophy and it was taken away from us. And for Notts, too, they had to score X amount of runs in so many overs. It was ridiculous how they got that as well. It was a hard one to comprehend.'

Compton can also remember the agony and disappointment of not getting over the line. 'It was just painful,' he said. 'When Nottinghamshire got the three wickets they needed, it was hard to watch. We thought we had a great chance. We had a great team; I'd say we had the best team. I guess Nottinghamshire will contest that … That Durham game was very disappointing. If it had not rained, then I think we would have won. And I think even going into the match, there was a lot of belief – there was an electricity in the club – that we were on the brink of something.'

Yet that something did not come as Somerset were left to ponder what could have been. 'I remember batting with Murali Kartik and we fell short of 400 to get the last batting point [against Lancashire],' said Willoughby. 'We were trying to get him on strike and I got run out, stupidly. And you just think that one point could have won us a Championship. But, ultimately, Notts won it because they had one more win then us. So, in theory, they deserved to win it. But it was a tough pill to swallow.'

And that pill became even tougher two days later at Lord's. After being sent in to bat by Warwickshire, Somerset were restricted to 199 thanks to Imran Tahir's five-for. It was a below-par score – and a frustrating one as they were well set to make a big total having been 176/3 in the 31st over. Although they gave themselves a chance of winning by taking early wickets to restrict Warwickshire to 39/3, an excellent performance from Ian Bell sealed the victory. He hit 107 as they reached the target with just one over remaining. Somerset had finished as runners-up in all three competitions. 'It's very tough to take, but we have to learn some lessons from what is happening,' said Trescothick after the match. 'There is a reason why it happens. You only have to look at the two guys from Warwickshire; Imran Tahir getting five to take the heart out of the game then Ian Bell showing the world-class player he is. That's what you've got to do if you want to be the best, you have to show it at crucial times. We've got to improve and try to emulate that.'

In hindsight, it could be suggested that Somerset were not mentally prepared for the final with it coming just days after their Championship loss. Warwickshire, on the other hand, were in buoyant mood having beaten Hampshire in their final red-ball match to seal their Division One status. They also had a physical advantage with three players not appearing against Hampshire. In comparison Somerset, who used the same 15 or 16 players all summer, made just one change for the final. No Somerset player would use this as an excuse, but it is hard to deny it made a difference.

'That very day [after the Durham match], or that very evening, we travelled to Lord's for the final and we lost that as well,' remembered Suppiah. 'So it wasn't a great couple of days. Between 2009 and 2011, we pretty much used the same set of players in all formats. We had a squad of probably 15 players and 80 per cent of them would play in all three formats. So a lot of players were still quite down about it and, it's probably an excuse, but perhaps it did affect us. Bell played a superb innings, but the emotions – and the travelling and all that – can run quite high. You probably don't have enough time to prepare for it. Whereas Warwickshire, I'm not saying they had more time to prepare, but they could have done more white-ball practice.

We were still in a Championship and the Twenty20 ... It could have played a part.'

Dibble, who was on the fringes of the team throughout the summer, believes using the same group of players in each format could have had a negative impact. 'This could have been a weakness, but the team during those few years – no matter what type of cricket it was – was the same team,' said Dibble. 'They were very used to playing with each other and everyone knew their role really well. I think that was a pro and a con in a way because you could argue that come the end of the season, they had all played a lot of cricket and that could have been counter-productive, physically and mentally.'

Hindsight is a wonderful thing, however, and did not change the fact that Somerset had come up just short in all three tournaments. Yet it had still been a marvellous season for the club. In the Twenty20 Cup, they had won 13 matches – more than any other side – and they had finished top of their group. And if luck had gone their way during that bizarre last over of the final, it would have been Trescothick picking up the trophy rather than Cork. Moreover, to lose a final by virtue of having lost more wickets is cruel – so much so the rule no longer exists. They had been equally as impressive in the ECB 40, winning ten of their 12 group matches – a return matched only by Yorkshire. Despite losing two finals, they had enjoyed a great summer of white-ball cricket.

They could also take pride in the fact they had become the closest Somerset team in history to win the Championship. They had come closer than the team of Richards, Garner and Botham. They had come closer than the class of 2001, the first Somerset side to finish second.

If they had achieved that result in 1977, when Kent and Middlesex shared the title, they could add that missing trophy to their cabinet. If they had just got one extra point here or there, or if Nottinghamshire had failed to get those three wickets at Old Trafford, they would have been triumphant. It was a tremendous effort from Somerset – and one they should be very proud of. 'It was a good season,' admitted Willoughby. 'It went down to the wire and there was just one point in it, in the end. And that could have been won or lost at any point in the season. But there were a lot of good, solid performances throughout the year.'

Although they did not win any trophies, 2010 has gone down in Somerset's history as one of the most exciting and memorable summers they have ever known at the County Ground. But for Trescothick, his captaincy and the bid to win a first Championship, it was just the beginning.

2012

End of an Era

AFTER COMING so close to winning all three trophies in 2010, Somerset continued to be competitive. Although they performed poorly in the Championship, losing seven matches as Lancashire were crowned champions, they again finished as runners-up in both cups. In the Twenty20 Cup, they sneaked into the knockout stage by qualifying fourth in the South Group before beating Nottinghamshire to reach Finals Day. They then laid some demons to rest in the semi-final by defeating Hampshire, but they could not beat Leicestershire in the final, finishing on 127/9 to lose by 18 runs. 'It's as disappointing as the other two really,' said Peter Trego, reflecting on a third consecutive Twenty20 Final defeat. 'It is the nature of Twenty20 cricket, unfortunately. There's little words to describe how you feel. It seems to be becoming a habit, which is a shame.'

In the ECB 40, Somerset again finished top of their group. They followed this up with a rain-affected win against Durham, but the weather was not on their side in the final. Although Jos Buttler – now a full England international – scored 86, they were dismissed for only 214. Surrey then scored 189/5 inside 28 overs, with Rory Hamilton-Brown making 78, to win via the Duckworth/Lewis method. It was Somerset's fifth consecutive loss in finals. Between 2009 and 2011, they had finished as runners-up in seven domestic tournaments. 'Jos Buttler's knock was class, the sort you'd expect from somebody a bit older,' said Trescothick afterwards, as he contemplated another near miss. 'He showed how good he can be. I always thought we were under par, maybe 20 short. And, as it was a fairly tough wicket, we were still in with a chance. But we simply didn't have enough runs on the board and Rory Hamilton-Brown batted well.'

Although they had suffered another defeat, it was a memorable performance by Buttler. One player who recalls it well is Steve Kirby, who had joined the club at the beginning of the season and had sacrificed a lot in doing so. 'I actually had a benefit year at Gloucester lined up, so it was a really difficult decision to move to Somerset,' explained Kirby. 'But I didn't want to have any regrets at the end of my career. They embraced me with open arms and I was really, really grateful they gave me the opportunity. All I wanted to do was play for England, personally, and moving to Somerset gave me a new lease of life. It cost me a fair bit doing it – writing a benefit year off – but I have no regrets whatsoever. In fact it was one of the best things I ever did.'

In the final, Kirby and Buttler shared a tenth-wicket partnership of 14, with the latter scoring all the runs. Kirby had the best view in the house as Buttler did his thing. 'Even at a young age, when Jos was coming through, it was obvious to me that he was going to be pretty special,' remembered Kirby in May 2019. 'He took complete control.

I was pretty nervous going out there. I was able to block out five or six balls from Yasir Arafat and he just went to town really and gave us a total which we could bowl at. He played really well. We were really confident when we went out with the ball. But they just got a good partnership, and then when you're down to less than four or five an over at that point, it was sort of a canter for them. We really had to go for them and they just pressed the accelerator.'

Although Somerset were gutted to lose another two finals, they had qualified for the Champions League thanks to their Twenty20 Cup exploits. The competition, founded in 2008 shortly after the inaugural edition of the Indian Premier League, saw the best Twenty20 teams in the world compete against one another. Somerset qualified for the first tournament in 2009 having reached the final of the Twenty20 Cup. Yet they did not last long and were eliminated in the second round having won only one match. No English teams competed in 2010 because it clashed with the end of the domestic season, but they were back in 2011 and so were Somerset. The tournament organisers did not think much of them or Leicestershire, however. Despite two teams from Australia, two from South Africa and three from India automatically qualifying for the group stage, the English teams had to go through a preliminary round. It was an insult to England's domestic game, although Somerset were not fazed. They beat Auckland Aces and Kolkata Knight Riders to progress before topping their group to reach the semi-finals. Although they lost to Mumbai Indians in the last four, it was still a remarkable effort.

Adam Dibble, who made his only two professional Twenty20 appearances during the tournament, remembers it as the best experience of his career. 'There was one in

2009 that I didn't go to, but obviously most of the guys did, so I heard a lot about it,' recalled Dibble. 'When you were playing in the summer, you knew what was at stake … A lot of the guys who went in 2009 said it was a bit of a dabble in international cricket, really, because you're playing against the best in the world. From a team point of view, we had to go through qualification first; play two games to get into the comp. We played in the 40-over final at Lord's and then flew out the next day to do the preliminary rounds. I think one of the boys took only one pair of pants because nobody had, not so much confidence, but an expectation that we were not going to qualify and we'd be going home in a few days and that would be our season over. And I think that really helped us in a way because there were no expectations, no pressure.

'At the start of it, Kieswetter and Jos weren't there because they were playing for England, so the team was sort of pulled together with Snelly [Steve Snell, the reserve wicketkeeper] and the youngsters. People like Chris Jones, who wouldn't have played Twenty20 cricket in the summer, but was suddenly needed. There were probably fewer egos around. It felt a bit more like guys having a crack and a bit of fun with it. And I think that really worked to our advantage … I didn't play for a little while, but I trained hard, performed in the nets and eventually came into the team for the game against Warriors, a South African team. I did well there, and we got through to the semi-final against Mumbai Indians. I did well there, too, so from a personal point of view it was great. I was contributing – I wasn't there to make up the numbers.

'There was a period in the middle where we didn't play a game for eight or nine days. And it was the end of the season as well. It had a bit of a stag do feel to it because everyone was thinking, "There's nothing to lose; we're not expected to do anything; we're playing against ridiculous IPL teams." It felt like we were letting our hair down a bit. We didn't have anything to stay fit for, so we were having some good nights out. That really helped the team spirit, as well … We were all just having good fun with it and lapping it up. With that inexperience and youth, you don't feel pressure; you don't feel nervous; you don't know what to expect, so I think that helped us in a way.

'It was a great experience. Out in India it's nuts. It was an ICC comp, so everything was business class – flights and five-star hotels – amazing. There were proper crowds; the crowd noise out there was ridiculous. And there were parties with Virat Kolhi and AB de Villiers and Mark Boucher. Getting to meet those kinds of players was nuts. Best experience I had as a player – and I think a lot of the guys who had a hell of a lot more experience and games for a longer period of time also quote that as a particular high point. In the past ten, 20 years of Somerset cricket, where a lot has been achieved, that is still high up there in a lot of people's memories.'

A more seasoned player who also rates the experience highly is Kirby. 'To go and be part of the Champions League was amazing, one of the best experiences I've ever had,' he said. 'We went to India with a very under-strength young side. It was a real testament to the way the group pulled together and the way the young players stood up to be counted. I thought Peter Trego was brilliant in the way he galvanised everybody … To go as far as we did in the tournament – finishing in the last four in the world – was one hell of an effort.'

And even George Dockrell, who has played in six World Cups across two formats for Ireland, has fond memories. 'I went out a little bit late because of some Ireland games, but it was an incredible experience,' he said. 'You're playing domestically but going out there and playing against some of the IPL teams, some of the best teams in the world. For me that was definitely one of the highlights of my career. I think it was invaluable to test yourself at that level.'

Somerset's performance in the Champions League was just the boost they needed going into the winter break. It was proof that their desire to win trophies and compete at the highest level had not diminished, despite all those near misses. Ahead of the 2012 season, they made a huge signing. Vernon Philander, the upcoming star of South African cricket, agreed to join the club for the first two months of the season. The seamer had made an impressive start to his international career during the winter, taking 51 wickets in his first seven Tests. With South Africa's tour of England approaching, Philander was keen to make an impression at Taunton. 'I'd like to get used to the conditions and get Somerset off to a good start,' he said.

Although they had signed Philander, Somerset had lost quite a few first-team players since September 2010. Before the 2011 season, Zander de Bruyn had left for Surrey and Ben Phillips had moved to Nottinghamshire. And there were more departures before April 2012. Murali Kartik had joined Surrey and Charl Willoughby, after six years of service, was released and signed for Essex. But he did not last long at Chelmsford, retiring at the end of the season. 'I think it was a good decision in the end for Rosey to let me go,' admitted Willoughby. 'I hadn't had an injury, literally, for ten years. I was getting a bit older and I think they wanted to bring some younger guys through, so I respected that. I went off to Essex and unfortunately got injured within the first six weeks and I, eventually, was forced to retire. I had a year left on my contract, but I just wanted to have an operation. At one point I was playing six months in South Africa and six months in England. At some point it's got to catch up with you.'

Although his time had come, Willoughby was a big loss to Somerset because, at his peak, he was a superb player. 'He was so important for years,' said Kirby. 'One hell of a bloke and an unsung hero.'

Dibble added: 'For someone who really only had one string to his bow – he couldn't really field, apart from throwing with his ridiculously good arm, couldn't bat and everyone knew what they were getting, a big in-swinger that's going to hit you on the toe – he was still able to perform and get people out for fun. His stats, I think he probably got 350 first-class wickets for Somerset. He was Mr Consistent with the new ball. Charl and Tommo were exceptionally skilled bowlers who could find out county cricketers pretty easily, especially Tommo in all forms of the game, Charl obviously a bit more in red-ball cricket. They were very skilled.'

Although they had lost some big players since 2010, Somerset still had a very good squad and a great chance of winning silverware. On the eve of the season, their fans had plenty of reasons to be excited.

* * * * *

Somerset's opening match of the Championship season was against Middlesex at Taunton. Their top order had not changed much since 2010. Arul Suppiah was still opening the batting alongside Trescothick and Nick Compton, James Hildreth, Craig Kieswetter, Buttler and Trego still dominated the middle order. Their attack looked a lot different, however. Philander was joined by Kirby, as well as Craig Meschede and Dockrell. Meschede, a 21-year-old all-rounder who had been educated at King's College in Taunton, had made his Championship debut against Sussex the previous summer. He offered Trescothick another seam option, while Dockrell, a 19-year-old from Dublin, was the team's new primary spinner. He had made a good impression the summer before as Kartik's understudy, taking two wickets on Championship debut against Nottinghamshire.

Missing for Somerset that day was seamer Gemaal Hussain, who had moved from Gloucestershire with Kirby in 2011. He had enjoyed an impressive season in 2010, taking 67 first-class wickets at an average of 22.34. Alfonso Thomas was also unavailable as, after years of impressing in Twenty20 cricket, he had bagged a deal in the Indian Premier League with Pune Warriors. He would miss the first six Championship matches. Despite missing two seamers, their new-look attack performed well in the season opener. Middlesex were dismissed for 246 with Philander picking up a five-for. In reply the hosts took control of the match. A big score from Compton – who was frustratingly dismissed on 99 by Toby Roland-Jones – and a valuable 83 from Kieswetter gave them a 104-run lead. Despite a defiant 50 from Chris Rogers, Middlesex were bowled out for 175. It was an impressive display from Dockrell, who claimed six wickets to confirm his place in the side. Needing just 72 for victory, Somerset comfortably got over the line thanks to an unbeaten 37 from Hildreth. It was the perfect start to the season.

Next up was a trip to Edgbaston. It was a tough start to the match for the visitors as, after winning the toss and electing to bat, they slipped to 14/3. They failed to recover from that desperate position, limping to 95/8 before a crucial 38 from Philander got them up to 147. Somerset's attack did fight back, however. Three wickets from Dibble restricted Warwickshire to 243. Although they were nearly 100 runs behind, they were back in the match. And thanks to knocks of 133 from Compton and 93 from Buttler, Somerset had something to defend. They made 354, leaving Warwickshire needing 259 runs for victory. It was going down to the wire.

For most of the chase, the hosts were in complete control. They reached 190/3 and victory was in sight. But then Trego turned the game on its head. He dismissed Darren Maddy, William Porterfield – who had made 84 – and Tim Ambrose to leave Warwickshire on 197/6. Kirby then dismissed Rikki Clarke and Trego picked up his fourth wicket, that of Keith Barker, as they slipped to 207/8. Suddenly the game was Somerset's to lose.

But then a brutal, counter-attacking innings from Jeetan Patel snatched the win for Warwickshire. He hit an unbeaten 43 off 36 balls to condemn Somerset to their first Championship defeat of the season. More importantly, however, they had missed a big opportunity. Although they had narrowly avoided relegation in 2010, Warwickshire were among the favourites for the title after finishing second the summer before. Somerset needed to be more ruthless. They needed to be winning these big matches. 'There was a game against Warwickshire, which we played pretty early on,' remembered Kirby. 'And we almost beat them. We had them eight or nine down and Jeetan Patel put on a really strong partnership at the end, which pulled it away from us. And that game now, looking back, was probably a game where we had a chance. He was dropped down at third man, but if we would have had him, things could have been different. You can't look back on situations like that, though.'

A week later, Somerset travelled to Trent Bridge. It was a frustrating affair as rain fell, but the visitors played brilliantly in adverse conditions. Bowling first, they dismissed Nottinghamshire for 162 as Trego claimed a five-for. It was yet another fine moment for the all-rounder, who was enjoying his talismanic role. 'I was signed by Somerset when I was 15 and straight out of school,' Trego told journalist George Dobell during the match. 'They give you your kit and your bats and you feel fantastic. But that was all taken away from me when I was 23. After that I had to scrap for a job and it made me realise how much the game meant to me. Once you have had to fight to get something back, you are much less likely to let it slip away again and I think the whole experience made me a better cricketer and a better person.'

It could have been a lot better for Somerset if it were not for Chris Read, who hit an unbeaten 104. In reply Somerset made batting look easy. Suppiah hit 124, Hildreth made 102 not out and Compton, continuing his good start to the season, scored an unbeaten 204. 'Somerset's batsmen applied themselves well and some of ours were responsible for their own downfall,' said Read. With time running out in the match because of the weather, Somerset declared on 445/2. Yet they were thwarted. They managed to dismiss only four batsmen as Read and a young James Taylor, who was closing in on an England debut, spared Nottinghamshire's blushes. 'The weather has done us a massive favour,' admitted Nottinghamshire's director of cricket Mike Newell. Rain had been the winner – and there was more bad news for Somerset. Trescothick had damaged an ankle tendon during the match and would not play again, in any format, until late July. It was a huge blow as they initially hoped he would be back by mid-June.

The injuries were starting to mount for Somerset. Hussain was still unavailable, Kirby was unable to bowl during Nottinghamshire's second innings and Philander missed the match because of a back problem. After using nearly the same XI for much of 2010, they were now being forced to frequently dip into their reserves. Ahead of their next match against Lancashire, 18-year-old twins Jamie and Craig Overton were named in the 12-man squad. The young all-rounders were quick, raw and had just been on England's Under-19 tour of Australia. 'We have had good reports about them from the recent England Under-19s trip and they are in contention,' said Rose before the match. 'We will make a decision on which of the twins plays shortly before the game when we have assessed conditions.'

And it was Craig who got the nod, dismissing former South Africa international Ashwell Prince for his only wicket. Yet Prince had already made 96 runs before that moment – and he was not the only South African to excel at Taunton. Philander had been passed fit to lead the attack and performed admirably, taking another five-for. His efforts were in vain, however, as rain again dominated proceedings. Most of the second day, large parts of the third and all of the fourth were lost. A draw was declared with Lancashire posting 400 and Somerset stranded on 87/3.

A day after the match finished, the Met Office confirmed April 2012 as the wettest for 100 years. Very few cricket fans were surprised by the news.

* * * * *

Somerset's ECB 40 campaign began against Surrey at the Oval before their next Championship match. Their attack was very inexperienced because of their mounting injury problems. Jamie Overton was making his one-day debut, Lewis Gregory, a promising all-rounder, was playing in just his ninth one-day match and Meschede was making only his tenth one-day appearance, although he had played in last summer's final. And that innocence told at the Oval as Hamilton-Brown hit a century to inflict more misery on Somerset. Surrey's total of 295/6 was always going to be tough to chase and they got nowhere near it, making just 190. It was frustrating for Trescothick, who was powerless to help his injury-stricken team. 'I think you're always concerned when you get a decent amount of injuries,' said Trescothick. 'We are in a situation where we are down to our last 11. There is no doubt it's tough and it's sad where it is at the moment. But it's professional sport and it's part of the job you go through. You're still going to get the same quality with the lads going out with the will to win … Come the end of the season it might be a little bit easier, as we might be a bit fresher.'

The defeat against Surrey was a nightmare start – and it only got worse from there. In their next match against Durham, they were bowled out for 208, 15 runs short of their target. On a more positive note, it was a day the Overton family will never forget. Craig made his one-day debut and Jamie picked up four wickets. The latter was omitted for the next match against Hampshire, although they could have done with him, as they took just one wicket. The game started poorly for Somerset when they lost Kieswetter, Trego and Hildreth, who was standing in as captain in the absence of Trescothick, and Thomas, for single figures. Half-centuries from Compton and Buttler got them up to 212/9, but that was nowhere near enough as Michael Carberry hit 103. Hampshire chased down the target within 29 overs to make it three defeats from three.

That soon became four from four in Somerset's final match before the start of the Twenty20 Cup. It was another under-par batting performance as they limped to 205/8 at Trent Bridge. That total was never going to be enough with an inexperienced attack bowling against the likes of Taylor, Alex Hales and Samit Patel. Nottinghamshire eased to victory with more than three overs remaining. It was a shocking start to their white-ball campaign, but there was some good news. Thomas was back from his spell in the Indian Premier League to captain the side and Kirby had recovered from injury, although they were still missing Trescothick's brilliance.

* * * * *

Somerset's Championship campaign continued with a trip to Chester-le-Street. And they got off to a flyer. Craig Overton claimed four wickets as Durham were knocked over for 125. Meschede also impressed with the ball, taking 3-26 during his nine overs. Somerset reached 220/8 in reply before the umpires called stumps on the first day. While it was not a big score, a lead of 95 put them in a commanding position. But then came the rain. No play was possible on the second and third days and by time play resumed, the result was a formality. 'It has been raining for the best part of 45 hours,' said BBC Newcastle's Martin Emmerson in the commentary box. 'But this now means Durham have effectively lost 11 days already this season to the elements and we are only into game five. I pity the brave souls who journeyed up here from Cornwall for this one.'

Thankfully, the weather improved for Somerset's next Championship match against Surrey at the Oval – and their top order made the most of the sunshine. Suppiah and Hildreth both hit centuries, Compton made 83 and Kieswetter just missed out on a half-century with 49. There was also a good knock from Alex Barrow, Trescothick's replacement. The 20-year-old, who had made his debut the summer before, scored a useful 47. It was a dream come true for him to play for Somerset and make a positive contribution. 'It was an ambition of mine to play for the club, since I was a young lad,' said Barrow, remembering his playing career. 'It's something I look back very proudly on. It was just great to play for my home club with some really good mates and people who I grew up admiring.'

Their efforts allowed stand-in skipper Hildreth to declare on 512/9. Surrey then began to chip away at the total. Steven Davies scored 104 and de Bruyn, facing his former team, hit 52. They were eventually bowled out for 388 with Philander taking four wickets in the final match of his stay. Surrey brought themselves back into the contest by bowling the visitors out for just 180. They needed 305 to win and Somerset needed ten wickets.

The fourth innings started well for the visitors as Philander dismissed Davies early on. But a young Jason Roy, promoted to open, scored 41 to frustrate them alongside South Africa international Jacques Rudolph, who made 45.

When they both fell, Surrey went for the draw. Gareth Batty produced a defiant innings – lasting 118 deliveries – before Hamilton-Brown saw them home with an unbeaten 70. Surrey had survived with three wickets in hand, leaving Somerset with just 11 points.

It was a frustrating result for Dockrell, Somerset's 19-year-old spinner. As their main spin option, the pressure was on him to win the match on the fourth day. He performed well, taking four wickets, but not well enough to force a result. 'I'm a little bit disappointed to be honest,' said Dockrell in his post-match interview. Yet he had to move on quickly as Durham arrived at Taunton for the next match. Thomas was back to play his first red-ball match of the season, a huge boost for Somerset, although he was powerless to stop Will Smith scoring a century as he and Michael Di Venuto put on 158 for the first wicket. When Thomas broke their partnership, dismissing Di Venuto for 96, and Buttler ran out Mark Stoneman for 27, a young Ben Stokes came to the crease. The 20-year-old hit a quick 60 off 79 balls to show why he was so highly rated. Durham had posted 384, which was not a terrible performance by Somerset after that big opening stand.

Trego, who picked up three wickets, then led the fightback with the bat. He smashed 89 and Compton, Hildreth and Craig Overton all made half-centuries to help Somerset declare on 400/9. And their recovery continued with the ball. Craig Overton dismissed Stokes for a fourth-ball duck before Dockrell, responding in the best way to his disappointment at the Oval, picked up six wickets to bowl the visitors out for 167. Victory was now in sight – and Somerset wasted no time in reaching their target. Thanks to Suppiah's 73, they knocked off the 152 runs required within 34 overs. It was a very impressive turnaround after conceding nearly 400 runs during the opening day.

Dockrell had benefited from Taunton's spinning conditions. In previous years, the County Ground was a difficult place to win matches because of its flat pitch. But during the 2010s it became more susceptible to turn, leading to the ground being christened 'Ciderabad' – a witty pun combining the Indian city of Hyderabad with the county's favourite alcoholic beverage. Somerset decided to start preparing more spin-friendly surfaces around 2010 when they realised seam was not quite doing the trick. 'There had been a lot of chat and a lot of working out on what to do with the pitch at Taunton for Championship games,' recalled Michael Munday. 'Taunton always had a reputation for being probably the best wicket for batting in the country. However, if all you are doing is drawing your home games, then that's probably not going to lend itself to you being promoted from Division Two or winning the Championship. In 2007, we decided to prepare wickets that were more seamer friendly.

'And that worked quite well, we tried to stick with that over the next few years … We played Hampshire in a game there in 2008. We wanted a result, so we poured water all over the wicket to make it seam and swing everywhere, lost the toss, got stuck in and were bowled out for 100 or something before lunch, James Tomlinson took an eight-for. But the game was still a draw because we had scored about 500 in the second innings because it was just the flattest wicket you'd ever played on. But that first game in 2010 … Murali Kartik wasn't there by that point, but he was coming. And there was a thought of, "We have some pretty good players of spin … How about we actually prepare spinning wickets at Taunton?" And in that game against Essex, which was rain-affected and a draw anyway, I probably bowled about 30 overs, which I wouldn't have been expected to be doing at that time of year.'

But contrary to popular belief, Somerset were not just preparing dust bowls. They were trying to create pitches that would allow batsmen to score, but also give bowlers a chance in the fourth innings. While he admits the conditions helped him, Dockrell does not believe they were overzealous in their preparations. 'The pitch itself was naturally flat, very tough for seamers to get much out of it, so I knew it was tough for the groundsman to create a pitch that was a good contest but then would actually still end in a result,' said Dockrell. 'Moving towards a pitch that offered something for the spinners helped do that, but it wasn't drastic. I never felt when I played it spun much on day one or day two, but it just gave it a chance to deteriorate towards the end of the game and that brings spin into the game. And I suppose the games we did win when I was there, a lot of the time, were games which looked like they might disappear into a draw and then things happened quickly on day three, day four. And I suppose that's what you want ideally in a Championship game.'

Next up for Somerset was a trip to New Road as Thomas, the club's official vice-captain, assumed the captaincy from Hildreth. It was a tough start for him with Worcestershire piling on the runs, 340 to be precise. Vikram Solanki scored an excellent century, but he was forced to share the limelight with Trego after he took five wickets. Yet there was bigger news as Compton almost made history. On 1 June, he reached 1,000 first-class runs for the season. If he had made it a day earlier, he would have become the first man to reach the landmark before the end of May since Graeme Hick in 1988. But he was denied by the weather as rain fell at New Road. As such, he joined Rob Key, who hit the landmark on 2 June, 2004, in the just-after-the-end-of-May club. 'It is all a bit of an anti-climax,' said Compton on 31 May, knowing he would not be following in Hick's footsteps. 'I must be honest, there have been a few sleepless nights thinking about the possibility of getting those thousand runs … I've been unlucky with the rain here today but in England you can never take the weather for granted.'

Although Compton did not get the chance to finish the job on 31 May, he did the next morning – and he took it with an excellent century. Half-centuries from Hildreth and Buttler, who made 85, also helped Somerset's cause. They had reached 253/4 before a collapse saw them dismissed for 298. Worcestershire's attack had dampened their hopes – and so had the rain. The game ended in a draw with Worcestershire finishing on 129/7 in their second innings. Yet there was some late entertainment. As the game faded into obscurity, Kieswetter removed the gloves, chucked them to Buttler and decided to have a bowl. He picked up the only first-class wickets of his career to finish with figures of 2-3. A stellar albeit slightly amusing effort. Although Kieswetter's bowling was a talking point, Compton dominated the headlines. For him to reach 1,000 first-class runs within the first 60-odd days of the season was an exceptional achievement.

It was proof that Compton had transformed himself from a promising talent into one of the finest batters in the domestic game. After regaining his place in the team, he enjoyed a great red-ball campaign in 2011, scoring

1,098 runs at an average of 57.78. 'In 2010, the last sort of five or six games made things very clear for me in my head,' said Compton. 'In the back end of the season, I had realised what I needed to do and how I was going to play. And that was enough of an impetus to then go into the 2011 season. I think there were a few technical changes as well, which I kind of learnt along the way. But there was no doubt that I had to put a marker down. Mentally, I knew what I was trying to do. I knew what first division cricket required, it was tough. If you're opening the batting or batting in the top three, it's not an easy place to bat in county cricket.

'For me, there was a real focus in the pre-season on my defence, building a world-class defence. If you have a world-class defence, you can bat for time. If you don't have a world-class defence, it's a lottery. You might hit some boundaries, but as soon as a good ball comes along, you're going to be out … And this wasn't just about preparing for county cricket, this was about preparing for an opportunity at Test cricket. My practice up until the start of 2011 was as elite and as forward-thinking as it had ever been, some of the measures that I went to. Batting in the dark and against a bowling machine at 100mph, making it very uncomfortable so I was much more resolute and could carry those emotions through, not just for one hour or two hours but for a whole day.'

Compton also had Darren Veness to thank for his good form. 'There was also the physical side of it,' continued Compton. 'Darren helped us become incredibly fit, the fittest I'd ever been. And I think it was a culmination of the hours I'd spent in pre-season that when I came into 2011, it was no coincidence that I did what I did. I probably stood a little bit taller halfway through that season as well, which enhanced my play of the short ball. Anything that was short, I became very good and scored at will off that. I also wasn't lunging at the ball as much, which made a huge difference in the way I played the ball; I played it a lot later. And I worked very hard at that.

'You put all those bits together and you had somebody who could bat time, who could keep his wicket. And as Brian Rose told me, "Just don't get out." With some players, if you told them not to get out, they would probably tense up and not move very well. But for me, it calmed me because I knew I had the shots ... But whenever I went out there and tried to play the shots, I then got very anxious. So if I just told myself to bat, the runs came naturally. That's how I built it up. And the following season, in 2012, that was my first real marker of a really good season. I knew that a lot of players could do it once – score a thousand-odd runs – but could you do it twice? And fortunately, I managed to do that.'

International recognition was now in sight for Compton. Somerset, however, still needed him to perform consistently if they were to challenge for silverware. Their next game was against Middlesex at Lord's, their final match before the Twenty20 Cup began. It was a poor batting display from Somerset, bowled out for 173. Hildreth top scored with 58, but he was one of only four to reach double figures. In reply Chris Rogers made 173 in a brutal exhibition. His colleague Joe Denly also hit a century as Middlesex declared on 364/3. Just as the match was slipping away from the visitors, rain descended on Lord's and they only needed to bat out the final day to secure a draw. Although Barrow completed his pair, Compton continued his good form. He finished unbeaten on 69, surviving 150 deliveries, to save Somerset. 'The weather has for once this season come on our side,' said Thomas after the match. 'But we've definitely been outplayed the last three days. Middlesex have bowled and batted better than us and we have to go back to the drawing board – try to fix things for the Twenty20 campaign coming up.'

* * * * *

Somerset were expected to do well again in the Twenty20 Cup after reaching the final three years in a row. Their campaign got off to a flyer at Taunton, beating Warwickshire by 63 runs. South Africa international Richard Levi, who had been signed especially for the tournament, enjoyed an excellent match. He hit 69 off 34 balls, with his compatriot and fellow Twenty20 signing Albie Morkel making 38. Signing Levi, who had burst on to the Twenty20 scene with a record-equalling high score of 117 against New Zealand in February, was a bit of a coup for Somerset. 'I think he will be a very exciting player for our supporters to watch,' said Rose, who would have been delighted with Levi's debut performance after missing out on his first-choice signings. Chris Gayle had withdrawn late on, as did his initial replacement, Faf du Plessis. Morkel was also a back-up when Roelof van der Merwe pulled out after failing to get a work permit in time. A big part of their squad during last year's tournament and the Champions League, van der Merwe was a loss. Yet Morkel, who had played for South Africa in all formats, was no mug – proven by his excellent debut.

After their win against Warwickshire, Somerset won four more matches to finish top of their group, with three lost to the weather. Those wins included a chase completed inside 14 overs against Northamptonshire and a score of 182/6 against Glamorgan. And there were some special individual performances. Hildreth scored an unbeaten 107 against Glamorgan and a young Max Waller picked up four wickets against Warwickshire. Waller, aged 24, had established himself as the team's first-choice leg-spinner since making his debut in 2009. Career-best Twenty20 figures against Warwickshire only confirmed his class. 'With the cricket we've played over the last three or four years, we breezed into quarter-finals and semi-finals,' said Rose after top spot was confirmed. 'But we've done it the hardest way. We started well but faltered, before coming back to play a very professional game ... We've learnt our lesson from one or two innings we've had in previous games and I thought we did very well.'

There was also another tremendous display from Buttler. Having been overlooked by England for the ODI series against West Indies, the 21-year-old hit 58 off 38 deliveries against Northamptonshire. 'Jos batted fantastically, so all credit to him,' said former Somerset all-rounder Cameron White after the match, impressed with the fine player Buttler was becoming. And there was Thomas, who had done a stellar job captaining the side in Trescothick's absence. Yet it could have been very different after he was almost persuaded to play for South Africa during their tour of England. 'A month-and-a-half ago, they wanted me to do a U-turn and make myself available for the Twenty20 World Cup and one-dayers,' said Thomas in July 2012. 'But there were a couple of speed bumps we came across along the way. At the age of 35 you have to think about family more than bright lights and glamour. It was one of those things where your heart said, "Yeah, do it." But after a couple of days to think it through, I thought that at my age it was too big a gamble.'

After a tough start to the season, Somerset were back on track with yet another excellent Twenty20 campaign. They had also won a match in the ECB 40 at long last. It was crucial that they overcame Scotland at the County Ground having lost their first four games and seeing their fifth washed out. Yet they did not bat convincingly. The visitors consistently picked up wickets with only Kieswetter making a half-century. Their score of 206 was not a huge amount, but it proved to be enough as Meschede claimed four wickets to bowl Scotland out for 146. They were back on track with a 60-run win and ready to take their new-found form into the Championship.

* * * * *

Somerset's first red-ball game back was against Warwickshire at Taunton and it was, arguably, their biggest of the summer. The visitors were beginning to run away with the title having won four Championship matches. Considering how many games had been lost to the weather in April and May, this was a striking return. If Somerset were going to stop them, they had to win. The match did not start in their favour, however, as only 10.4 overs were possible during the opening day. And when the rain disappeared, Warwickshire made hay. Skipper Jim Troughton and Chris Woakes, a year before he won his first Test cap for England, scored hundreds. They were eventually bowled out for exactly 400. After impressing with the bat, Warwickshire hammered home their advantage with the ball. Jeetan Patel took a seven-for as the hosts were dismissed for 254, with Compton scoring an unbeaten 73 and Suppiah making 54. Trescothick's absence was continuing to be felt.

But Somerset fought back through Hussain. He picked up his first five-wicket haul for the county as they dismissed Warwickshire for 124 on the final day. They now had a slim chance of victory after being behind for most of the fixture. They needed 271 to win, knowing a draw would not be good enough to get them back into the title race. And their chase started poorly. Barrow, Suppiah and Hildreth were all removed with just 15 runs on the board. But then came something special, as Kieswetter joined Compton at the crease. With Compton batting at a steady pace, scoring 52, Kieswetter went into white-ball mode. He hit a spectacular century to drag Somerset towards victory. When he was dismissed for 152, Somerset were just 12 runs away from their target with four wickets in hand. They were made to sweat when Keith Barker dismissed Meschede, Thomas and Waller to leave them nine down. But Trego got them over the line with Hussain supporting at the other end. Somerset had snatched victory to move eight points behind Warwickshire. The race was on.

Somerset's next game was against Lancashire at Aigburth in Liverpool, one of the country's most famous outgrounds. Making his Championship return was Trescothick, much to the delight of everyone connected with the club. While he was making a much-needed comeback, 21-year-old Jack Leach was making his maiden Championship appearance. The left-arm spinner made his first-class debut four months earlier against Somerset for Cardiff MCC University, but failed to take a wicket from his 41 overs as Compton and Hildreth both scored double centuries. With Somerset bowling first, Leach would have been keen to open his first-class account at the second attempt. But he was given just one over by Trescothick as the seamers ran through

Lancashire. Thomas and Trego both took four wickets as Lancashire were bowled out for 185.

Lancashire's attack responded brilliantly, however, to dismiss Somerset for 149. Not even Compton could make a decent score as he fell to Simon Kerrigan for 22. Despite the low totals, two days had passed by the time the hosts had started their second innings because of some poor weather. When they did get under way, they struggled again and were only saved by Ashwell Prince's 129. But it was a special day for Leach, who claimed his first two Championship wickets. Prince's effort had got Lancashire up to 242 and with Somerset requiring 279 to win, it was game on. But rain on the fourth day ended both teams' hopes with Somerset on 93/3. It was a frustrating draw for all involved. 'It's been a pretty hard-fought game all the way through,' said Trescothick, perhaps slightly relieved to avoid defeat. 'It was evenly poised, although it may have been more in their favour than ours with the scoring rates in the game. But who knows what could have happened if we'd have got a partnership together?'

Somerset's next match was against Nottinghamshire at Taunton and they desperately needed a win to keep their title challenge alive. It was the same situation for the visitors, who were pushing for a second title in three years. Somerset were without both Kieswetter and Compton after they were selected to play for England Lions. Nottinghamshire's Patel had also been selected. Although Kieswetter was a big loss, Compton was their form batsman. 'We're where we are in the table mainly because Nick Compton has played so well in adverse conditions,' said Rose, commenting on his call-up. 'It's frustrating to get towards the end of the season and have a clash of fixtures … But I'm a great supporter of England Lions games because it's a precursor to Test cricket. Nick deserves to play and all credit to him, he's played tremendously well.'

It was a massive game for both sides, yet the British weather did not get the memo. The first two days were almost completely washed out, with Nottinghamshire reaching 48/3. They were eventually dismissed for 156 as Hussain took four wickets. In response Somerset were unable to reach 400 and claim maximum batting points. Hildreth scored 83, but no one else made a noteworthy contribution. They were dismissed for 249 before Nottinghamshire finished the match on 176/5. As Somerset were left to curse the clouds, Warwickshire eased past local rivals Worcestershire to extend their lead at the top. The title was slipping away.

The next team to visit Taunton were Sussex. More rain fell on the opening day, ending play at 3pm. Sunny skies made a rare appearance the next morning, allowing Trescothick to score a much-needed century. It was his first since his double hundred against Worcestershire in July 2011. More importantly, it was the 50th first-class century of his career. 'I didn't sleep too well last night, knowing I was on the verge of my 50th hundred and it's a proud day for me,' said Trescothick.

It was the kind of quality innings he was known for at the County Ground. While he had played at the highest level, Trescothick did not find the county game easy. He worked hard to ensure he could always give everything to the cause, even though the carrot of international cricket was no longer dangling in front of him. 'He's a legend of the game,' said Kirby. 'It was a pleasure to watch the way he used to go about his business. His work ethic was probably one of the best I've ever seen. And his fitness, too. You could say he's probably not the most athletic bloke in the world, but he would never, ever stop on his fitness. He was always trying to be better than he was the day before. This one time he was 70 not out at lunch and he came in, threw his lunch down his neck and went to the nets before he went back out. And I was like, "Tres, what are you doing?" He said, "I'm out of nick, Kirbs." And I said, "Out of nick? I wouldn't mind being out of nick on 70 not out!" But that was him all over.'

Talent aside, Trescothick's outstanding work ethic is something many of his former colleagues have highlighted. 'Marcus Trescothick is an extremely talented player,' said Johann Myburgh, who joined Somerset in 2014. 'He's obviously retired now, but in my mind he's the best English batsman I've seen in my era. Marcus has spoken openly about it, but it's a shame that he couldn't have played more international matches for England because I think he would have held many records. He sets a high standard, in terms of work ethic. He loves the game. Having shared an opening stand with him on numerous occasions was an absolute privilege. And picking his brain about batting was nice to do.

'He hit more balls than a lot of people at the age of 40. If I think about some other players during my time as a cricket player, once they started getting to the end of their careers, they knew what their game was about; they were looking after their bodies; they might have not hit as many balls as they did as a youngster. Whereas Marcus, that was certainly not the case. And that's just part of who he was and how he got into his comfort zone and how he went about preparing. Some people don't need to hit that many balls, some people are different. A guy like Peter Trego possibly didn't need to hit as many balls as Marcus to get his game into shape or get mentally ready. Marcus was hard-working, but in my mind exceptionally talented.'

One person who worked a lot with Trescothick behind the scenes was Veness. He recalls the time when the two tried to improve his game before the 2011 season. 'In 2010, Somerset qualified for the Caribbean Twenty20,' explained Veness. 'There were a couple of academy lads that didn't go on the tour [which took place in January 2011], but other than that it was just me and Tres that stayed back. And we had about three weeks where it was me and him, one on one, and it ended up being one of the best moments … To be able to have that quality time with him. He took his training to another level from that season. He almost had a second wind from a physical point of view. Even now, if you stick him on two wheels on a bike, he'd take most of the lads!'

It was important for Trescothick to maintain his high standards as Somerset's captain and talisman. He was very much someone who led by example, showing the younger players, such as Dockrell, how to succeed. 'I grew up watching Marcus Trescothick playing, so getting over there and actually playing with him and seeing how he went about it was pretty incredible,' said Dockrell. 'His work ethic was next to none and he was on his own with how much he loved cricket; just a pure, absolute love of it.'

Trescothick is passionate about helping youngsters improve for the benefit of their careers and the club, which is why he moved into coaching once his career finished in 2019. 'At the time [when I was there, he was] a 40-odd-year-old who'd done everything in the game,' said Jim Allenby, who joined Somerset in 2015. 'And he's still doing the things that academy players are doing, in terms of the way he's training and the way he's helping players out around the club. If he's finished having a bat in the nets, he'd be throwing balls to people and things like that. That really stood out to me – how much he was willing to give to other people when he wasn't focusing on his own game. And subsequently he's joined the coaching staff, which is absolutely fantastic ... I didn't really know what to expect from him, but I was absolutely shocked. I just thought he'd be the Somerset legend who did what he wanted; had his bat and sat down. But what he gave to the environment and the players and the team was phenomenal to watch and something I have a huge amount of respect for.'

Michael Bates, who also joined Somerset in 2015, added: 'I've genuinely never met anyone who loves cricket as much as he does. For someone who has played for so long and has been through a lot, it's well documented and he's spoken about the amount he went through from a mental perspective. I played second-team games with him and he would treat it no different to a first-team game. He would be out of form and he'd go out to bat and properly grind out a 50 to try and get himself back in form, to try and get himself back in the first team. And he was around 40 at that time. He's an absolute legend, but for him to still have the passion and the love and the desire to keep improving, to keep succeeding at that point in his career was incredible.'

Trescothick's work ethic had paid off against Sussex with a century. But he did not get much support from his team-mates as Monty Panesar took 7-60 – his best first-class return – to restrict them to 247. Sussex, who were also battling for the title, then struggled as Abdur Rehman took control. The Pakistan slow left-armer, who had signed for the second half of the season, took his first five-for for Somerset. He would go on to play a crucial role during the remainder of the campaign while Dockrell was captaining Ireland at the Under-19 World Cup. 'He has an excellent first-class record, with a bowling average not dissimilar to Murali Kartik's,' said Rose on signing him. 'He has played in 16 Test matches for Pakistan, the latest in Sri Lanka being only last week.'

While Rehman's arrival was good news for Somerset, it was indifferent news for Dockrell. He went on to make just one more Championship appearance that summer, all but curtailing his season. Yet to get the chance to play consistently at such a young age, finishing the season with ten Championship games under his belt, is something he cherishes. 'It was a funny season for me because it got broken up,' said Dockrell. 'Starting the season so well – we'd gone top of the table having won two at home against Durham and Middlesex – and for me playing a part in those wins was absolutely amazing. Being whatever age I was and taking those wickets early season was unexpected for a lot of people and a little unexpected for me, thinking early season I wouldn't get a look-in … It was a pity then I did go away. Obviously the Under-19 World Cup was a fantastic experience, but it was a pity not to have played more of a part through the rest of the season. But to see Abdur Rehman come in and do what he did was pretty incredible.'

Another newbie playing for Somerset was Sajid Mahmood, who had been signed on loan for the rest of the season. The Lancashire quick, who had made eight Test appearances for England, had joined to ease their mounting injury problems. Thomas was missing with a hamstring injury, Meschede's finger was playing up and Gregory had a side strain. 'We have signed Saj because of the experience he can provide at a time when we are short on troops,' said Rose. One of the reasons why Somerset were getting so many injuries was their commitment to each format. Years of playing their best players week in, week out – not to mention their ageing squad – was starting to take its toll. 'If we look at between 2009 to 2012, four years on the bounce of competing in all formats with the same group of lads, it's inevitable that takes a degree of a toll,' explained Veness.

To make matters worse, Mahmood went wicketless on debut as Sussex reached 279 thanks to an unbeaten 57 at No.9 from former England seamer Amjad Khan. They then quickly ended Somerset's second innings. Panesar took six more wickets, as Suppiah was the only half-centurion. They were dismissed for 195, leaving Sussex needing just 164 to win. But Panesar and his colleagues were denied by the weather on the final day, finishing on 115/5. It was a result which neither side wanted as Warwickshire, having salvaged a draw, remained top. 'It was a rubbish day,' said a frustrated Trescothick after the match. A week later, the Met Office said that 2012 was the second wettest summer since records began. With Warwickshire grinding out results, Somerset's title hopes were sinking quickly in the Taunton puddles. Time was running out.

* * * * *

Despite their Championship woes, Somerset were still going strong in white-ball cricket. They had put a run together in the ECB 40 following their win against Scotland, defeating Durham, Glamorgan, Nottinghamshire, Hampshire and Scotland again to make it six consecutive wins. Much of their success was down to Trego, who was enjoying an excellent tournament. With the bat, he scored 245 runs at a strike rate of 130.31 – a rate only bettered by Durham's Phil Mustard (minimum five innings). And with the ball, he took 15 wickets at an average of 24.80. Just nine bowlers were more prolific. Buttler was also performing well, scoring 289 runs at an average of 41.28. To qualify for the semi-finals, they needed to win their final match against Surrey and hope that Hampshire lost their game with Durham. Surrey brought a strong squad to Taunton. Roy was opening the batting, Kevin Pietersen was making a rare appearance, and former Somerset stars de Bruyn and Kartik were also involved. It promised to be a huge game, but the weather did not relent. Rain washed out the match and they were knocked out in the most frustrating way imaginable.

But rain did not hamper their progress in the Twenty20 Cup. In their home quarter-final against Essex, they posted a solid score of 175/6 as Hildreth made 58 off 36 deliveries. They then bowled their opponents out for 148, with Gregory putting in a breakthrough performance. Although he conceded 39 runs from his three and a half overs, he took the final four wickets – including that of Ryan ten Doeschate, who was well set on 47 – to finish the match. It was a victory that confirmed their place at a fourth consecutive Finals Day. 'It almost feels like a habit going back to Finals Day,' said Hildreth after beating Essex. 'It's wonderful for the club that we've managed to get back there. We've got a really good team here. We seem to be peaking at the right time and seem confident in this format. If we keep remembering the things we do well, then hopefully we'll go one step further.'

Somerset's opponents in the semi-final were Hampshire, their conquerors in 2010. The match got off to a poor start. Levi was dismissed for one and, even more damaging, Hildreth scored one off eight balls. Trego, coming in at No.6, followed that trend as he made one off seven. Balls were being used up at an alarming rate. Kieswetter offered some respite with an unbeaten 63, but their total of 125/6 was never going to be enough to see off Hampshire. Some good bowling from Somerset's attack slowed down their opponents' strike rate, but they eventually got over the line with six balls to spare to seal a comfortable six-wicket win. 'It's a dreadful feeling,' said Trescothick afterwards. 'You put so much effort in, so much blood, sweat and tears but at least we keep putting ourselves in the position to be shot down. We will continue to do the hard work and we will get it right. We have based our club on a lot of hard work and we're good at what we do, but we just need to get a bit better. On the day we were just not good enough and we were outplayed by the better side.'

Hampshire had beaten Somerset at Finals Day for the second time in three years. Although Somerset had knocked them out in 2011, Hampshire wicketkeeper Bates believes they had a mental advantage. 'For whatever reason we tended to have the upper-hand on them,' he claimed. 'And it felt like we played them all the time. Any big game, any knockout tournament, we'd come across them at some point ... Every time we came up against them, we respected them hugely. But I think we were always quietly confident and knew that because we'd done it several times before, we felt confident we could roll them over again.'

And that experience of consistently beating an opponent – in big matches – cannot be overstated. Losing a big match can improve a player as they do not want to endure the pain of losing again. A fine example of this is Ben Stokes's man-of-the-match performance in the 2019 World Cup Final, coming three years after Carlos Brathwaite hit him for four consecutive sixes to win the 2016 World T20 Final. But it can also have a negative effect, mentally scarring the player. And perhaps this was the problem with the team Rose had built at Somerset. Trescothick, de Bruyn, Thomas, Kartik, Willoughby and Kirby were all in their mid-30s, while Suppiah, Hildreth, Compton and Trego were not exactly young. Only Kieswetter and Buttler were blessed with the fearlessness of youth.

Somerset also played the same team in all formats. There were few opportunities for young players to break into the side, with some, such as Meschede, Gregory and Dockrell, getting a chance because of injuries. In the years since, Somerset have put more faith in their superb academy. But back then, they failed to get the right balance of experience and inexperience in the side. This is something Dibble, one of the young players who was trying to force his way into the team at this time, picked up on. 'A big thing which counted against us a lot in those years was the same team played almost every single game, no matter what the format was,' he said. 'I don't think a lot of the young guys got enough opportunities; whether or not we deserved them is a different argument. But I think in the last few years some of the young guys have been given a chance and a run of games, even if they hadn't necessarily performed in the second team, although a lot of the time they had ... I don't think there was enough trust in the young guys for them to go out and perform.'

And maybe it was their lack of youth which caused them to falter when it really mattered. Somerset's experienced team knew how to perform consistently throughout the season, which is why they were competitive in all formats. But did they miss that fearless edge a young player, without the scars of yesterday, can bring? Should they have asked some of their older players to step aside in white-ball cricket? It was something they benefited from in 2011 when they reached the Champions League semi-final. Considering how Somerset began to actively promote their youngsters in the years that followed 2012, perhaps that was the biggest lesson. Bates believes Hampshire's fine balance of young and old is what made them so successful between 2009 and 2012, winning four major trophies.

'That period that I was involved in at Hampshire brought us a huge amount of one-day success,' said Bates. 'And looking back now, I think our team had a brilliant balance between us young lads, who just gave so much energy, enthusiasm and passion to the team, and the likes of Dimitri Mascarenhas, Dominic Cork, Neil McKenzie and Sean Irvine – huge amounts of experience that we were able to feed off, but also provide stability to guide us when we needed it. I think role clarity within that team as well was really clear and evident. Everyone knew what their job was. And more often than not we went out and executed it – it was as simple as that. Momentum is a funny thing and we just kept going, confidence just built, and on our day we felt as if we could beat anyone.'

The third of Hampshire's four trophies during this period was the 2012 Twenty20 Cup as they defeated Yorkshire in the final, before going on to beat Warwickshire in the ECB 40 final a few weeks later. Somerset were left to ponder how Hampshire were able to win plenty of one-day trophies, while they came home with only runners-up medals. With Warwickshire picking up result after result in the Championship, their chances of winning silverware in 2012 now looked very slim.

* * * * *

Shortly after losing to Hampshire, Somerset were back in Championship action. Surrey were the visitors at Taunton in a match which saw the best of Pietersen. The mercurial batsman was playing for his county after he was dropped by England following the 'Textgate' scandal, in which he allegedly sent insulting messages about his England colleagues to friends in the South Africa team, who they were playing in a three-match Test series. Pietersen responded to his axing with an excellent 163 against Somerset, helping them post 317. 'Kevin Pietersen was simply magnificent on the opening day at Taunton,' said BBC London's Mark Church in the commentary box. 'He batted as only he can and dominated proceedings, mixing the sublime with the outrageous, and he looks in prime form, as he has done all summer.'

After no play was possible on the second day due to rain, Somerset began clawing back the deficit. Hildreth made 85, Trego made 92 and Jones made exactly 50. Their innings came to an end on 294, although not without controversy. With Barrow on 12, Kartik ran him out at the non-striker's end for backing-up too far – a practice more commonly known as 'Mankading'. It was a horrible moment for Barrow, who had been struggling to find form. Tasked with filling in for Trescothick for large parts of the summer, he finished the season with just 186 first-class runs at an average of 12.40. On the face of it, it seemed as if he was a young man who had failed to take his chance in professional cricket. But that was far from the truth. Barrow had been struggling with a shoulder problem before being selected. Because Somerset were already missing plenty of players through injury, he did not say no to a first-team chance. It was a tough situation for Barrow, one which only got worse as the season progressed.

'I had a shocking year and, to be fair, one I probably never recovered from, from a mental aspect,' admitted Barrow. 'At the start of the [calendar] year I was really looking forward to it. I put myself in a really good position the year before; scored a lot of second-team runs and came in at the latter end of the season. I think I played six or seven games and did all right opening the batting, averaging just under 20. I started to feel quite confident playing first-team cricket and I felt there was a route for me to develop into an opening batter. And then came 2012. I went to Australia at the end of the 2011 season and then came back in January 2012 for a shoulder operation. And I can remember being up at Hove when Tres got injured. I can remember being quite concerned about it because I knew I wasn't fit enough to play first-team cricket because of my shoulder operation. I hadn't had enough time to recover and I was pretty certain I was going to be the person to go up [and replace Trescothick].

'You naturally have that selfishness as a sports player, thinking, "Right, I'm the best person for this job." But I also knew I wasn't fit enough to do it, which was a big concern. And then I played in a one-day game and got 72 on debut. Then we went down to Surrey and I got 40-odd quite quickly and played really nicely. And I suddenly thought, "I can do this; I can manage my shoulder; I can still bat." Then things started to spiral out of control pretty quickly and, unfortunately for me, we weren't in a position where we had enough people to come in. So even though I wasn't doing well, I wasn't able to be dropped either which, in hindsight, was a bit of a nightmare because sometimes you just want to get out of it – you want to get away – and I couldn't. It just kept on doing more and more damage the more I played.

'Kieswetter and Jos were playing for England, Tres was injured and I think the squad was only 19 or 20. We didn't have a big squad. So, it was one of those things where if you had a squad of 25, you're sort of more under pressure for your place. I can remember playing in second-team games and there would only be two professional cricketers playing. So that just shows you how small the squad was and how a few injuries can really hinder second-team cricket – and have an impact on the first team because you have a smaller pool of players to pick from.'

The toughest moment of his summer was undoubtedly the incident with Kartik, which came just as Barrow was getting the chance to bat lower down the order at No.6 and make some runs. As you would expect, he had the full support of his club and skipper. 'It's not what you come to expect in county cricket – I've never seen it before,' said Trescothick at the end of the day's play. 'That was quite astonishing and disappointing. The game doesn't need to come to that. It's not the game we like to play. It annoys the players and upsets the players.'

Former Gloucestershire wicketkeeper Steve Snell, who was part of Somerset's 2011 Champions League squad, added: 'I've never seen anything like it in my nine years in the professional game. Kartik was very well respected at Somerset – he was a very good cricketer – and Alex Barrow is the nicest of players. It's really bad sportsmanship and I'm shocked by it, if I'm honest. He was acting within the laws of the game but it's an unwritten rule that you just don't do it – especially in the four-day game. I know there was some ill feeling. I can't see how he isn't embarrassed when he looks at what he's done. As a cricketer, you wouldn't think about doing it.'

Despite criticism from his former club, Kartik remained unapologetic. He believed Barrow was cheating and trying to gain an advantage. 'If a batsman is out on a stroll in spite of being warned, does that count as being in the spirit of the game?' wrote Kartik shortly after the incident on Twitter. He was defended by his captain Gareth Batty, who upheld the appeal. He did apologise for bringing the game into disrepute, however. 'The last thing I wanted was to bring the spirit of cricket into disrepute,' said Batty after the incident. 'In the heat of the battle I made the decision that, according to the letter of the law, was the correct decision for him to be out ... People obviously think the spirit of the game has been brought into disrepute – that was not my intention and I thoroughly apologise for that.'

And because 'Mankading' incidents dominate the cricketing news whenever they happen, a lot of big names waded into the debate in support of Kartik. 'You don't leave [your] ground until [the] ball is released,' wrote David Lloyd on Twitter. Although plenty were defending him, it was tough for Barrow, a youngster just making his way in the game, to be painted as a cheat. The debate had been diluted down to whether 'Mankading' was in the spirit of the game. It became dehumanised, with critics forgetting that an inexperienced 20-year-old – not accustomed to the limelight – was at the centre of all of this. Every pundit or social media user who came out in support of Kartik was another blow to Barrow's confidence and reputation. The same could be said about Kartik, yet he was a 35-year-old who had experienced far greater scrutiny while playing for India. He was more accustomed to handling the situation. It was not easy for the youngster to keep calm and carry on.

'The worst thing about that was the timing of it,' said Barrow. 'I was obviously having a pretty stinking season and I was really battling. I remember having a net with Andy Hurry about playing Kartik. He was one of the first real quality spinners that I had faced and I didn't really know what to do or how to play it. So we went down, hit a few balls and said, "Right, I've either got to sweep him or I've got to use my feet." I had a go at sweeping and didn't really like that so I decided to use my feet. I went out clear in what I was going to try and do and I actually felt like I was doing well and playing him nicely. But it was a weird game; a weird atmosphere as well between the two sides before it happened.'

Perhaps the hardest thing for Barrow was his family going through the ordeal with him. 'It was more annoying for my dad,' he added. 'That was the thing that sort of worried me the most – how the emotion carried to my family. I was in disbelief, to be honest. But I can remember our physio coming up and saying, "Baz, your dad's down there." So, I called dad and was like, "Dad I'm round here, do you want to meet me?" Just to try and take the emotion out of it. If I chat to dad about it now, or it comes up, he'll growl and curse just because of how it happened … If you watch any game of cricket, what I was doing happens every ball of every game. It wasn't a case of trying to steal yards or anything like that, I was just backing up. And you back up in rhythm with the bowler, so you leave the crease as the ball leaves their hand. One of the worst things was when I was watching the TV and getting called a cheat by the Sky pundits … If you analysed Alastair Cook doing this in a Test match, he'd be in exactly the same position. I can remember sitting at home with my mum next to me and mum was like, "Oh my God, this is awful.'"

To this day, Barrow struggles to understand why Batty decided to uphold the decision and why he was criticised so heavily by the media. 'It was incredibly frustrating and in hindsight I wish I stuck up for myself a little bit,' he admitted. 'I was like, "I've got Kartik here, I've got Gareth Batty there. I'm a young lad and going to put my head down." And I think also I was like, "Surely they're not going to uphold this appeal?" But the mood Kartik was in; he was getting angry at Tregs; he was just on edge. And obviously there was a bit of history because he left Somerset the year before on not great terms. I just looked at Batty and thought, "He's not going to say yes to it!" And the umpire asked him three times, "Are you sure you want to uphold this?" And he said, "Is he out?" And the umpire said, "Yes – are you sure you want to uphold it?" And he said, "Well if he's out, yes." And then he asked him for a third time, "Are you sure you want to do that?" And in the end the umpire said, "Sorry Alex, that's out." And obviously that's when the booing started coming as people started to realise. I didn't actually walk into the changing-rooms, I walked into the gym. I just didn't know what to do. I was embarrassed; I was angry. I didn't know how to react to it, to be honest.

'It's not cheating from a bowler's perspective and I don't think it's cheating from a batter's perspective; you move in time with the game. The problem comes when it's used in spite because it's just a cheap wicket. If you're in a tight run chase and someone's halfway down the wicket, for me, if I was playing against them, I'd say, "Look, I think you're taking the mick here and I really don't want to have to get into a situation where that happens, so just be respectful." And if that happens and someone keeps doing it, you probably don't have a choice. It's when it's completely out of the blue and a really cheap way of gaining an advantage [that it becomes wrong]. Think how far batters are out of the non-striker's end when someone drives a straight ball back and the bowler gets a touch on it. If you're thinking that's going down at 90 miles per hour and coming back at a similar pace, you've got probably 0.6 seconds between the ball being released and contact – and people are two or three metres out. It's not cheating, you're just in rhythm with the bowler.'

The incident overshadowed the match and remains an infamous moment in Somerset's recent history. It did not define Kartik's career, his eight Test caps did that. But it defined Barrow's. Whenever another 'Mankading' incident occurs in the world, such as Ravi Ashwin's dismissal of Buttler in the 2019 Indian Premier League, he is reminded of that strange, distressing moment in his career. 'If it happens in the world, I'll get a Tweet about it,' said Barrow. While the media already had their headline, the match still needed to be finished. Surrey's second innings confirmed the draw as Pietersen hit 58 and Arun Harinath made a century. Nine Somerset players had a bowl in that innings to try and entice Surrey into a declaration, including Buttler, who produced 12 deliveries. To this day, it remains the only two first-class overs of his career. But the two sides could not agree on a declaration. 'We couldn't work it out,' said Trescothick after the match. 'We offered, they offered but we couldn't agree.'

There was a similar result at Edgbaston, minus the controversy. Warwickshire had defied Nottinghamshire as Tim Ambrose scored an unbeaten 151 to secure a draw. They now had one hand on the title – and it was just a matter of time before they had two. Although their title challenge had faded, Somerset still had two matches to play and could secure second place. Their penultimate game came at Hove and they enjoyed a good start. Rehman and Thomas picked up three wickets each as Sussex were bowled out for 221. But their hopes were quickly squashed by Panesar and his colleagues. The England spinner took three wickets as Somerset were bowled out for just 134. Trescothick and Jones were the only players to score 30 or more. Their misery was further compounded by Chris Nash. The Sussex opener hit 126 as they posted 308 all out, meaning the visitors needed 396 to win.

It was an almighty challenge, but Somerset rose to it. A big first-wicket partnership of 147 between Trescothick and Suppiah gave them a good start before an unbeaten century from Hildreth and an excellent 89 from Trego saw them over the line. But as Somerset celebrated the second-highest successful first-class run chase in their history, Warwickshire were celebrating something much bigger at New Road. They had beaten Worcestershire by an innings and 202 runs to claim their seventh Championship title. 'It couldn't have gone any better for us on the final day,' said Warwickshire skipper Troughton. 'It's been a great effort all season and is a deserved reward for all the work we've put in since last year. It's a proud moment for me to get my hands on that trophy again. I probably took it for granted when we won it in 2004, when I was a youngster, but this win means the world to me.'

With the title gone, Somerset were keen to win their final match of the season against Worcestershire as they looked to end Rose's tenure as director of cricket in style. Rose was stepping down after overseeing one of the most successful periods in the club's history. He had made the decision to leave after they suffered their fourth consecutive Finals Day loss at Sophia Gardens. 'I have come to the conclusion that a fresh approach is needed at first-team level,' said Rose as the news broke. 'I will continue to try and assist the club in meeting its core objective of winning trophies. Somerset is extremely well placed to prosper in the future and I look forward to seeing this magnificent club go on to even greater things.'

Although they had picked up just one major trophy during his tenure – the 2005 Twenty20 Cup – Rose had transformed Somerset's fortunes and built one of the best teams in the club's history. And for that, he deserved a lot of credit. 'Brian has served the club with great distinction as a player, captain and as the director of cricket,' said chairman Andy Nash. 'He has transformed the performance of the first team, taking them from the bottom of the second division to one of the most consistent and competitive sides in all three competitions.'

A win against Worcestershire at Taunton would probably secure a second-place finish, a great way for Rose to sign off. The match started well for the visitors with Daryl Mitchell and Phil Hughes putting on 74 for the first wicket. But when Rehman dismissed Hughes for 42, a remarkable performance unfolded. Rehman finished with career-best first-class figures of 9-65 as Worcestershire were dismissed for 212. The man to deny him a perfect ten was Trego, who had Chris Russell caught behind for the eighth wicket. 'It was a fantastic day for me,' said Rehman. 'When a fast bowler takes wickets like that, no one says a thing. When the spinner does that, they say the pitch is no good!'

In response, Somerset dominated with the bat. Trescothick scored 146 and Compton, who finished the season as the Championship's highest run-scorer with 1,191 at an average of 99.25, hit an unbeaten 155. It was a performance that secured his place on England's tour of India during the winter. He made his debut on the subcontinent as a replacement for the retired Andrew Strauss. Unfortunately for Compton, he would become the first of many replacements for Strauss as England struggled to find their next opener during the succeeding years. Somerset's innings finished on 512/9 as they declared in search of a big win. The match ended quickly with Worcestershire bowled out for 152. Rehman picked up another five wickets to finish with 14 in the match and 27 for the summer at an average of 14.18. Somerset were left to ponder how prolific he could have been if he had played the entire season, not just four Championship matches.

The result had confirmed second place, the third time Somerset had achieved that position in their history. Although they had failed to clinch the title, they could take solace in the fact they were beaten by a far better side in Warwickshire. They were always two wins away from challenging the eventual champions and having won their final two matches of the season, they could be proud of beating Nottinghamshire, Sussex and Middlesex to the runners-up spot. 'We finished second, but we probably didn't deserve to be second,' said Barrow. 'We had a real late surge when Rehman came in and propelled us up there. I think the feeling among us was that we were second, but we had not been consistent enough or challenged to win the Championship.'

And perhaps that is why Somerset could not win a trophy during this period, the fact they were always beaten by a better team. When you look at their eight second-place finishes in all competitions between 2009 and 2012, there were times when they were unlucky. No doubt, the Twenty20 Cup Final and the last few minutes of the Championship season in 2010 will always strike a chord with Somerset fans. But a lot of the time, they were completely outclassed by their rivals, such as when Warwickshire stormed to the title in 2012.

While it is impossible to ignore their near misses, Hurry appreciates the strength of their opponents. 'The reality is we were beaten by better teams,' he admitted. 'We showed some really good progress. The year Durham won the Championship and we played Lancashire here [at Taunton in 2008], I think they were fifth in the Championship and they beat Kent to leapfrog everybody and win it. That was one of the first years where we were in that position and it was managing that expectation and pressure associated with it. Don't get me wrong, we got ourselves in a position where we tied the Championship, when Notts won it by just winning more games than us. We did come second a lot; we did take some learning from it. Don't forget that final down at the Rose Bowl in the Twenty20 where that very last ball from Zander de Bruyn, with the aid of Hawkeye, we know that was lbw and not given out. We also know that if we had the opportunity again, we would think differently and run the striker out. We weren't that far away!'

As for 2012, two of Somerset's biggest challenges were the weather and the wickets – a horrible combination for teams looking to win games. Warwickshire managed just six wins all season and four of them came before June. That figure looks stark when you compare it to other title winners. Lancashire had ten wins in 2011 and Durham had eight in 2009. It was the first time since 2008 that a team had won the Championship with just six wins. The pitches were particularly tough at Taunton, where only half of the matches ended in a result. 'The pitches were remarkably flat,' remembered Kirby. 'It was very difficult to get 20 wickets and to win at home. You were playing to the last hour, the last half an hour of Championship games at Taunton. And they were such gruelling games to produce wins from, really.'

Yet the conditions were the same for everybody in what was a hard summer of county cricket. What really killed off Somerset's hopes in 2012 were injuries and absentees. Only seven members of the squad managed to play at least ten Championship matches with Trescothick, Thomas and Kirby all missing seven games for one reason or another. In total, 24 cricketers played Championship cricket for Somerset. In comparison 16 players appeared for them in 2010, 12 of whom made at least ten appearances. The lack of a settled team was their biggest problem.

Rose's departure marked the end of an era for this great team, one which should have won a major trophy. During the next few years, various players left the club. One of the first was Suppiah, who was forced to retire in 2013 with persistent problems in both knees. He was just 29. 'I am devastated to have to retire from the game that I have always loved,' he said at the time. 'This is the hardest decision of my life, especially having played for Somerset for so long ... Somerset will always be my county and from the other side of the boundary ropes, I shall continue to support the lads in every way I can.'

And he was not the only premature retiree, as Kieswetter called time on his career in 2015. At 27, he was even younger than Suppiah. And it was a horrific way for an excellent career to end. While batting in a Championship match the previous summer, Kieswetter was struck by a delivery from David Willey. The ball went through the grille of his helmet and hit his right eye, fracturing his cheekbone. He returned to action a couple of months later, but his vision was not the same. Knowing it was unlikely that he would reach the heights of 2010 again, when he was man of the match in a World T20 Final, Kieswetter decided to retire. Cricket was left to ponder how much he could have gone on to achieve. 'I came back and played a few games and got through on adrenaline and support,' said Kieswetter shortly after his retirement. 'I played a Twenty20 comp and realised that physically my eye wasn't quite right. When you have a physical thing, it affects you mentally and you start to question yourself and your ability. There is a muscular injury but going through that trauma has pushed me back mentally. As a person, if I can't give 100 per cent then I'd rather not let myself or the team down. It's disappointing and tough but necessary for me.'

Kieswetter's retirement would have paved the way for Buttler to become Somerset's primary wicketkeeper. But he had already left the club. He had decided to move north and join Lancashire before the 2014 season. And in fairness to him, he was never going to get a chance as wicketkeeper with England if he remained second choice at Taunton. Kieswetter was one of the best wicketkeeper-batsmen in the world and showed no signs of regressing. 'Lancashire have an exceptional coaching staff which will help me to continue to develop as a wicketkeeper-batsman,' said Buttler on joining the red rose county. 'I want to pay a special thanks to everybody at Somerset. I thoroughly enjoyed my time there and will leave with plenty of good memories.'

And Buttler was not the only big-name player to make a high-profile transfer. A year after his departure, Compton, the glue that held Somerset's top order together, re-joined Middlesex. The last big player to leave in the years that succeeded Rose's departure was Thomas. Having taken more than 550 wickets across all formats for the club, he departed at the end of the 2015 season as one of Somerset's greatest bowlers. While he may have been at the peak of his powers during Rose's tenure, he still enjoyed plenty of special moments afterwards, including a hat-trick against Sussex in 2014 when he took a club-record four wickets in four balls. 'It's been great fun but like all good things they eventually come to an end,' said Thomas, reflecting on one of the best periods of his career. By the spring of 2016, the only surviving members of the 2010 side were Trescothick, Hildreth and Trego. A new era, without Rose, had begun. It was now someone else's job to try and claim their maiden Championship title.

2016

Rogers's Resurgence

BRIAN ROSE'S replacement as director of cricket was South African Dave Nosworthy, who was tasked with rebuilding the squad. Although he did not have much of a playing career, making just 29 first-class appearances during the late 1980s and early 1990s, Nosworthy had an impressive coaching CV. After coaching Titans in South Africa, he went to New Zealand and achieved plenty of success at Canterbury. Under his guidance, they won the Plunket Shield – New Zealand's domestic first-class tournament – as well as the one-day and Twenty20 competitions. He later returned to South Africa to coach Lions, but did not win a trophy and resigned in 2012, just a few months before succeeding Rose.

During his first season at Somerset, Nosworthy did not make any major signings. And that proved to be an unwise decision as they struggled in the Championship, finishing sixth and winning just three matches. It was a narrow escape; they only survived the drop thanks to victory in their penultimate match against Surrey and Derbyshire's loss to Warwickshire in the season's finale. Somerset fared better in white-ball cricket, however. In the ECB 40, they finished top of their group before eventual winners Nottinghamshire knocked them out in the semi-final. They also progressed in the Twenty20 Cup, although they could not reach a fifth consecutive Finals Day as Surrey edged past them in the quarter-finals.

Overall, it was not a great year for the club and one which Trescothick was glad to see the back of. They had struggled to compete in red-ball cricket for the first time since Langer's departure. 'We've obviously been very poor in our Championship cricket this year,' said Trescothick at the end of a season in which he had failed to score a first-class century. 'I'm so glad this season is done. It's been pretty demanding and pretty tough … We underperformed, underachieved and just had to keep grinding; probably different to where we've been competing for victories and being right at the top of the table … We've held on by the skin of our teeth and we're still going into it next season, so it will give us the opportunity over the winter to reassess, debrief and look at all the things to try and improve on and get right for next time.'

The winter saw some new faces arrive at the County Ground. Josh Davey, a Scottish international, was brought in from Middlesex. With only three Championship appearances under his belt, the 23-year-old was a signing for the future. They also signed Derbyshire bowler Tim Groenewald. The 30-year-old seamer had become an experienced county professional since making his Championship debut for Warwickshire in 2006 and was expected to perform week in, week out. 'I am absolutely delighted to be joining Somerset, as it is a club I've held in high regard for many years,' said Groenewald. 'I couldn't be happier committing the next three years to the club and I can't wait to get started.'

And there was Johann Myburgh, a batting all-rounder who had played all over the world. Myburgh started his career in his native South Africa, before moving to Canterbury in New Zealand and then to England to play for Hampshire and Durham. Yet he had not played first-class cricket for a couple of years before joining Somerset. During 2013, he captained Sutton in the Surrey Championship. Nosworthy, who had worked with him in South Africa and New Zealand, offered Myburgh a big opportunity to make a name for himself in English cricket. 'Mybs is a quality person and a quality professional cricketer,' said Nosworthy on signing him. 'His track record speaks for itself and I have no doubt that his experience and expertise will add massive value and depth to the team. However, he is coming to the club with no guarantees or any expectations, so I look forward to him fighting his way into contention.'

Despite these signings, Somerset endured a taxing 2014. As Yorkshire won their first Championship title in 13 seasons, they again finished in sixth place. Unlike the previous year, when a late flurry saved them, their form dropped off with no wins coming after July. Although they were not losing every week, it was an apathetic end to the season – as if there were nothing to play for. And their white-ball campaigns were not much better. In the new One-Day Cup – a 50-over competition that replaced the ECB 40 – they won just three of their eight matches. They also failed to get out of their Twenty20 group, winning only six of their 14 games in the newly rebranded Twenty20 Blast. With the team regressing, Nosworthy stepped down from his position at the end of 2014 – a year earlier than planned. 'I believe the time is now right for me to return home with my family for a number of personal and business reasons,' he said. 'I've really enjoyed my time at the club and it will always have a special place in my heart.'

Few were surprised by the decision considering the first team's poor form. 'It doesn't seem to have been a particularly happy camp over the last couple of seasons,' said Steve Snell while commentating on a match. The culture Rose, Justin Langer and Andy Hurry had instilled had deteriorated with their departures. 'There was a two-year period when the club was slightly disillusioned,' said Compton, who admitted he had been struggling with depression towards the end of his time at Somerset. 'There wasn't the same feeling in terms of the dynamics and the culture at the club ... I'd been dropped by England and was in a three-bedroom house on my own and I didn't know where things were going. The club's performance was imperative to me being down at Taunton and I realised that I was 30, 31. If I wanted to play for England again, I had to make a move to give myself the best opportunity ... When I then played against Somerset, I did find it hard because a lot of my heart was still there. It almost upset me that I left, just like that.'

The man tasked with rebuilding the team was former England batsman Matt Maynard. A previous director of cricket at Glamorgan, Maynard had plenty of experience. He was England's assistant coach when they regained the Ashes in 2005 and had coached in India and South Africa. 'The spine behind the club is really solid and they're all good people – that's what really impressed me,' said Maynard on taking over. 'It's exciting times. They've got a number of good young players alongside the skilled senior players. Now it's down to me to create an environment for them to reach their potential and that's certainly what I'll be trying to do.'

Maynard's first big signing was Jim Allenby. The all-rounder, who had previously played for Leicestershire and Glamorgan, had more than 6,000 runs and 250 wickets to his name in first-class cricket. 'I'm looking to win trophies and play in the most successful style and type of cricket that I can,' he said. But they got nowhere near to winning silverware in 2015. They again finished sixth in the Championship, recording just four wins – the same as relegated Sussex – and their safety was only confirmed during the last match with a victory against Warwickshire. In the One-Day Cup, they failed to get out of their group as they won four of their eight games. And in the Twenty20 Blast, they managed just four wins; no team won fewer in the tournament. 'I'm a little bit shell-shocked,' said Trescothick after they had lost their opening three Championship matches, a run of form which summed up the season. 'We haven't performed anywhere near the level we expect as a team … We've got some soul-searching to do.'

Despite the doom and gloom, there were plenty of positives to take from the season. Tom Abell had progressed to the first team after coming through the academy. The Taunton-born all-rounder, who was named *Wisden's* Schools Cricketer of the Year in 2013, had a breakthrough summer with the bat, scoring 726 Championship runs at an average of 36.30. Craig Overton and Lewis Gregory both had good seasons with the ball, taking 43 and 38 Championship wickets respectively, and so did Jack Leach, who, after a slow start to life as a professional cricketer, was beginning to flourish. He picked up a seven-for in the final match of

120

the season to confirm Somerset's safety. While they had lost some big-name players after Rose's departure, Somerset's emerging talents were proving the future was bright at the County Ground – and evidence their stellar academy was beginning to pay dividends.

Somerset's academy began to prosper under the leadership of Jason Kerr during the mid-2000s as they started developing high-quality local players such as Buttler, Gregory and Leach. For Kerr, his aim was to produce England internationals. 'Within the Somerset environment, we're incredibly fortunate in terms of the support we have,' said Kerr. 'My aim was to produce international cricketers and a by-product of that would be they play for Somerset for a long time. We had to aim higher. We had to create an environment that was far more challenging and was trying to recruit not only the best players, but the right characters; young players that certainly enjoyed the idea of having a growth-mindset, wanting to get better and were very aspirational to go all the way and make the sacrifices to get there.'

One of the reasons why the academy has had so many successful graduates during the last 15 years is the amount of time they invest in the youngsters. They try to make them feel like they are already a professional cricketer; that they are just as important as Trescothick or Hildreth. 'They've had real success in producing players through the academy,' said graduate Alex Barrow. 'Not all of them have stayed, but the percentage of players who have gone on to get professional contracts is very high. And certainly, when I was in the academy, the culture that Jason created was very similar to what it was like in the first team. And you recognise that when you make that transition, it isn't that different.

'That made the transition pretty straightforward. And now there's a lot more integration, a lot more fluency between academy and professional staff. You're a massive part of the club when you're in the academy. When you're 16 and in the academy, you think, "Cool, I'm in the Somerset academy, this is great." But actually, you're part of the club. You're training properly; you're training regularly; you're looking to be a professional cricketer. I think Somerset does it well. And the coaches and players they have are very good, but also very driven to play for Somerset and for England.'

The academy also benefits from the club's strong connections within the local community. They have an excellent relationship with Millfield and King's College, two of England's finest cricketing schools. Somerset work with these independent institutions to ensure they are doing all they can to help talent develop. 'I think community links are crucial,' said Phil Lewis, director of sport at King's College. 'When an academy is set up and runs as well as it does, but has the links ourselves and Somerset have created, it means there's a mutually beneficial process there. It means the players' programme, that runs either at the academy or at the school, runs side by side so they're always communicating and thinking about what is best for the players. I think the last thing you want is a school environment working on one thing and Somerset working on another. Also, the time that the players get now. At King's they generally stay with us and are boarders, so they get a lot of contact time at the nets. And then the contact time at Somerset in the academy has increased massively as well.'

But Somerset's community ethos is about more than just working with local schools and paying close attention to their young players. Developing talented cricketers is ingrained in the club's identity. Although they enjoy seeing global stars play for them, they love it when a Somerset lad breaks into the first team and succeeds. 'A club like Somerset is made by the people who are there,' said Barrow. 'That's what the club thrives upon and the members thrive upon – Somerset boys playing for Somerset. It's great having these good overseas signings and they come in and make an impact. It's great to share their experiences and add to the quality of the team. But it's so good having Hildreth who's been there for years; Trescothick; the youngsters who come through the academy – Leachy, the Overton boys, Lewis, Dom [Bess], George [Bartlett] – there's loads of people who have been at Somerset since they were 12, 13 or 14 years old.'

And the fact that Somerset have built such a great academy helps them attract players from across England and beyond. Current first-team cricketers Tom Banton, Ollie Sale, George Bartlett and Eddie Byrom were not born in Somerset or the surrounding counties. 'When you're a club that's doing well and has a good reputation, then you can also attract good young players,' said Michael Munday. 'Tom Banton's not from Somerset, he's from Warwickshire. But when players like that are looking for opportunities elsewhere, when you've got a club who are doing all the right things and have a good reputation, success breeds success, to some degree.'

While Somerset have continuously produced first-class cricketers, they have not always given them a solid run in the first team. When Rose was director of cricket, the same 14 or so individuals were playing across all three formats. But under Maynard, there was a real emphasis on getting the youngsters into the first team by playing them in the One-Day Cup. 'The chief executive Guy Lavender, Matt Maynard and myself sat down and we actually mapped out that we wanted to get guys like Lewis and the Overtons and Tom Abell a regular spot in the 50-over team,' said Allenby, who captained the one-day side in Alfonso Thomas's absence. 'That was a deliberate attempt to encourage the younger players to have a bit more of a voice and an influence in the team. It also helped that they are fantastic players. There was a real line drawn in the sand in 2015.

'That first season doing the One-Day Cup was challenging because I didn't know the players that well. However, we went into that competition with a really great mindset. As a project that went brilliantly. All the bowlers knew, before game one, which games they were going to play and which games they were going to open the bowling in or bowl at the death. Being a club with such strength all over, but especially in its bowling department, meant a couple of the younger guys hadn't been exposed to the pressure of the important overs. As a club we decided we were going to give opportunities to players in different batting and bowling situations and that went absolutely fantastically. We ended up winning our last four games that season having lost our first three. We really came out of that with some momentum for the end of the Championship season.

'That competition, for me, was quite a big moment … There was a bit of a vacuum, not only in talent, but also in personalities – the really big, domineering personalities – so there was a real emphasis to get these guys in the team and subsequently it's shown it's worked. Under Chris's [Rogers] captaincy they flourished and are now genuine match-winners and international cricketers. I can't speak highly enough about the Overton twins, Lew Gregory, Jack Leach, in terms of the way they have taken that opportunity to be match-winners. And not only match-winners, but their personalities and their attitude to the game is something I certainly loved. I love seeing them do well.'

For the incumbent director of cricket Andy Hurry, giving young players the opportunity to play first-team cricket is a huge part of the process. It is not the most important, however. 'It starts right at the very bottom, at grassroots level,' said Hurry, explaining how Somerset's academy gets results. 'I think the great thing about this club is it's very connected from the professional level to the grassroots level. We have great relationships with our National Counties partners – Devon, Dorset, Cornwall – and we have a really good, collaborative system that enables us, through good communication with those National Counties partners, alongside our own Somerset development pathway, to recognise the highest potential players in our region, create opportunities for them within our environment to find out more about these players, make informed decisions and then get them in our academy.

'Then we have the right expertise, people who are experts at working at that level, developing those guys and providing them with opportunities in our second team. And then we start to see the players are ready to get some exposure in first-team cricket. It's about being brave; demonstrating courage and giving them a go. I think there are a lot of clubs that have that philosophy, but there's only a small amount that have the courage to throw these young blokes in. But make sure they've got the right support around them; it's okay for them to get a taste and go back into second-team cricket and work on those areas.

And when they do come back in, they're more established. That process has worked really well because now we're not only seeing guys establish themselves in Somerset's first team but going on to play international cricket.'

Although the 2015 season had failed to deliver any trophies, for Maynard, that summer was more about understanding the team and what it needed to succeed. 'We basically tried to play in a style that suited Somerset,' said Maynard. 'With the toss coming into play, in terms of no toss, the side batting last won the vast majority of games and we had to try and change that; the wicket wasn't breaking up. After the first year, seeing 400 being knocked off twice in the last innings to win a game, I spoke to the chief executive Guy Lavender and the head groundsman and said, "Look, we've got to try and do something." The first year was always about trying to learn about the team, learn about the individuals within the team and what made them tick. And then the second year was all about pushing on – who did we need?'

The answer was Chris Rogers. The Australian had plenty of Championship experience following stints at Derbyshire, Leicestershire, Northamptonshire and Middlesex. After playing just one Test match before the age of 35, the 38-year-old had enjoyed a renaissance. He had cemented his place in Australia's top order, scoring five Test centuries, before calling time on his international career after the 2015 Ashes series. Still a fine player, Rogers was a brilliant signing for Somerset. But Maynard did not just want him for his batting. After six seasons as captain, a shattered Trescothick, now aged 40, had served his time. Somerset needed a new man in charge and Maynard saw Rogers as the perfect candidate. As such, he was appointed their new four-day captain and Allenby was put in charge of both white-ball teams. 'I will be giving Chris and Jim my unconditional support, as well as focusing on scoring as many runs as I can in the season ahead,' said Trescothick as the news broke. He would remain the first-choice opener.

And Maynard, along with the appeal of playing in the region, was pivotal in persuading Rogers to join the club. 'It came down to Matt Maynard,' recalled Rogers. 'He was looking for a captain and someone who could lead them. Marcus had probably said that he was happy to let someone else take the reins and just take it in a bit of a different direction. I just felt like I had one more year to give and it seemed to match up well with what was happening at Somerset and particularly with my initial years having played in Devon at the same club as the Overton boys, there was a pretty strong connection there. I have such great memories of my youth there that I just always thought it would be a great place to play.'

With his skipper in place, Maynard set about completing his squad. Leach became their first-choice spinner as Dockrell was released and he bolstered that department with the signing of Roelof van der Merwe on a two-year contract. The all-rounder, who had played international cricket for South Africa and the Netherlands, had re-joined the club following his Twenty20 stint five years earlier – only this time he was available to play in all formats. It was quite a coup for Somerset. 'I enjoyed my time in Taunton and I am really looking forward to working with Matt Maynard again,' said van der Merwe. 'For me to be coming back to Somerset to contribute in all forms of the game is awesome.'

With van der Merwe committing his future to the club, Maynard now had a squad that could compete again. '[We needed to] get someone to lead the side because Marcus was an unhappy skipper, if you like, and we needed someone who could still have a lot of drive and ambition left in their game,' explained Maynard. 'Chris Rogers came along, a really good, experienced player that obviously knew how to captain spin, which we thought was going to be vital with the very promising Jack Leach. We made the call that Jack was the future rather than George Dockrell, who was there when I came to the club. And then we obviously saw the emergence of a young Dom Bess as well. We signed Roelof van der Merwe for the white-ball [team] alongside Max Waller. We just needed to get the wickets to a position where they would spin and therefore make it possible for the fielding side to win in the fourth innings, as opposed to virtually impossible … We changed that, adapted that, and in Chris we had a great leader who gave it a real good challenge in 2016.'

With a new captain, some excellent signings and several talented youngsters emerging, it was an exciting time to be a Somerset supporter. Yet the media did not expect them to challenge for silverware. *The Guardian*'s Ali Martin envisaged an eighth-place finish in Division One while *The Cricketer* predicted they would end up one place higher in seventh. They had been written off by the press, but with Maynard being able to implement his masterplan, a gritty Australian at the helm, and a new team just emerging, they believed they could do something special.

* * * * *

Somerset's Championship campaign got under way at the Riverside Ground in Chester-le-Street. Durham, who had last won the title in 2013, still had a formidable team

Justin Langer, pictured here celebrating Somerset's promotion from Division Two, transformed them into one of the best teams in the land. He retired in 2009.

Craig Kieswetter looks at Marcus Trescothick as Warwickshire hit the winning runs in the 2010 ECB 40 Final. The result ensured Somerset finished as runners-up in all three domestic competitions in 2010.

James Hildreth was the highest run-scorer in the Championship during the 2010s, yet he has never played for England at senior level. He was at his best during 2010, scoring seven first-class centuries.

Somerset reached the semi-finals of the now defunct Champions League in 2011, the best performance by an English side during the competition's brief history. A young Jos Buttler watches a delivery from Lasith Malinga of Mumbai Indians.

Nick Compton averaged 99.60 in first-class cricket during 2012 and was called up to the England Test squad. He was Somerset's stand-out player that summer.

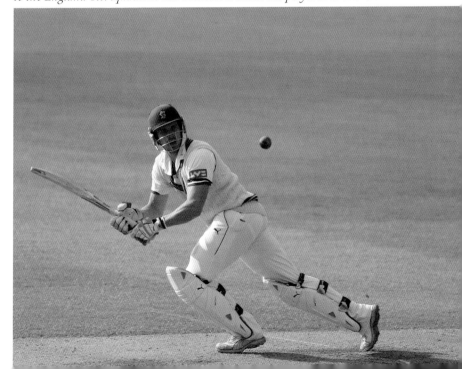

Director of cricket Matt Maynard and captain Chris Rogers revitalised the team in 2016 following a few apathetic years, narrowly missing out on winning the Championship.

The Somerset squad watch the title decider between Middlesex and Yorkshire in 2016. If the match had finished in a draw, Somerset would have been champions. Middlesex won with just 4.4 overs remaining.

Jack Leach enjoyed a breakthrough season in 2016, taking 68 first-class wickets. He celebrates their home victory against Nottinghamshire that summer with club legend Peter Trego.

Twenty-two-year-old Tom Abell was appointed captain in December 2016. It was a brave call by Matt Maynard, but he has since become the focal point of Somerset's brilliant young team.

Jason Kerr (left) and Andy Hurry (right) were appointed head coach and director of cricket respectively in December 2017. They have both been associated with the club for many years and are crucial to their success.

Rikki Clarke celebrates taking the wicket of Tom Abell at Taunton in 2018. Surrey's team of internationals outplayed Somerset during the 2018 title race.

Somerset celebrate their 2019 One-Day Cup triumph at Lord's, ending a 14-year wait for a trophy. During that time, they had finished as runners-up in ten tournaments.

Tom Abell enjoys their cup win with Brian Rose, who played a crucial role in regenerating the team during his tenure as director of cricket.

Somerset could not defeat Essex at Taunton in 2019 to win the title. The retiring Marcus Trescothick received a guard of honour and a standing ovation at the end of the match, with everyone honouring one of England's greatest cricketers.

that included Mark Stoneman, Keaton Jennings and Paul Collingwood. It was not an easy opening match, yet the visitors started well. They consistently picked up wickets throughout the opening day as Gregory finished with 4-58. They struggled to stop Jennings, however, as he hit 116 to help Durham post 256. Somerset then struggled with the bat. Trescothick was bowled by former England man Graham Onions for three and Abell, his new opening partner, was dismissed by Chris Rushworth for ten. And it was not a good match for Rogers either. He was run out for just 23. They were bowled out for 179, saved from an embarrassing total by Peter Trego's 45. That brought Jennings back to the middle. He hit another century, this time finishing unbeaten on 105, as Durham began coasting towards victory.

But luck was on Somerset's side as two days of rain descended on Chester-le-Street. The match was washed out and they had escaped with a draw, although Rogers was far from happy. 'Our fielding was top class and our attitude was top class but we disappointed with the new ball and that's pretty unforgivable at Durham in the first game of the season,' he complained afterwards. 'But the guys who had that ball in their hands will know that and they will get better. We found it hard with the bat and lost wickets in groups … I've learned a lot about the guys and there is plenty to work on. There is a lot of talent in the squad but how they put that into practice out in the middle is going to be our challenge.'

Somerset again failed to make use of the new ball in their next match at the Oval. Opener Rory Burns scored 80 and Kumar Sangakkara, the great Sri Lanka left-hander, hit 171. There were also half-centuries for Jason Roy and Zafar

Ansari as Surrey made 463. It was a particularly tough innings for Craig Overton, who finished with figures of 1-114. In response the visitors performed better with the bat. There were good knocks from Trego, Gregory and Craig Overton – who all posted 40s – and one special innings from Trescothick. He hit 127 to get Somerset up to 353 and keep them in the contest heading into the final day. They then bowled much better in Surrey's second innings. Craig Overton bounced back from his earlier struggles to pick up a three-for as the hosts declared on 181/8. And it could have been much better for them if it were not for Sangakkara, who made an effortless 71. It was a knock which forced the visitors to bat out the rest of the day. Poor efforts from Abell and van der Merwe did nothing to calm the nerves. But a much-needed display from Hildreth, now aged 31, did. He scored an unbeaten 40 as Somerset made it two draws from two.

Next up for Somerset were Lancashire at the County Ground. The opening day was another tough one for their attack. Lancashire declared on 493/9 in their first innings with Liam Livingstone scoring an unbeaten 108 and Steven Croft making 94. No one performed well for Somerset as Jamie Overton conceded 105 runs without taking a wicket. The bowlers were failing to deliver. In reply Somerset had to deal with James Anderson. He removed van der Merwe and Trego without scoring, as well as ending Rogers's innings on 55. But there was a masterclass from Hildreth, who hit 130. It was the sort of innings his skipper loved to see him play. 'Hildreth was a class act,' remembered Rogers. 'To see him go about, he's such a relaxed guy. And the way he batted – when he was on, it was a joy to watch.'

Paul van Meekeren, a Dutch seamer who joined the club ahead of the 2016 campaign, is also a huge admirer of Hildreth's composure. 'One regret of mine is that I probably didn't pick their brains as much, especially someone like James Hildreth,' he said. 'I'd never actually heard of him before I joined Somerset, which is quite funny because me being Dutch and home-grown and having always lived here, you don't really follow the County Championship and stuff. But just realising his record and just the cool and calm guy he is within the changing-room and just doing his thing. He's an incredibly funny guy as well, so you don't feel pressured when you talk to him.'

And Hildreth was not just calm with the bat. As Darren Veness reveals, he ticked off the hard yards in training with ease. 'A natural athlete, ridiculously talented,' said Veness. 'He was ridiculously casual at how he went about his business, but he could practically do anything. He'd run ten kilometres in a ridiculous time. He'd jump, he'd sprint and get some of the best scores. Then you'd see him in the gym doing all the work he needed to do and just casually sort of brushing it off.'

Feeling calmed alongside Hildreth was Jamie Overton, who made 51 at No.9 to help them reach 313. But that was not enough to avoid the follow-on as Somerset were left fighting for a third consecutive draw. The two that saw them home were Trescothick and Rogers. Trescothick, facing 254 balls, hit 129 and Rogers, facing 199 balls, made 75. Both players finished unbeaten as Somerset comfortably survived with eight wickets in hand. Although it was another unconvincing display, they were showing plenty of resilience and desire as they remained undefeated. 'Marcus and Chris played so well, but we mustn't forget

James Hildreth's century in the first innings,' Maynard told the press. 'Again, we have shown character as a team to pick up our third draw against a very good Lancashire side. Now we have to try and get ahead in a game so we can exert pressure.'

Somerset did manage to get ahead in their next match against Warwickshire at Edgbaston thanks to a much-needed knock from Abell. The youngster, who had failed to reach 30 in his previous four Championship innings, hit 104 as wickets fell around him. It completed a great 24 hours for Abell, who had been tipped as a future England player by former head coach Andy Flower. 'I've been struggling a bit lately but when you hear praise from someone like [Flower] it's incredibly flattering and pretty special,' Abell said. 'It was a very special feeling to get stuck in today and reach that landmark. It's a relief as I've not been pulling my weight so far.'

Trego's 94 got them up to 295 – a good score considering the pitch was doing plenty. Jamie Overton and Gregory then picked up three wickets each as Warwickshire were restricted to 152. And wickets continued to fall as the pitch became harder to negotiate. Abell, Hildreth and Gregory all fell cheaply but, thanks to Trego's 51, the visitors just about managed to reach 178. As the second day came to an end with Warwickshire's second innings under way, the result looked a formality. It seemed unlikely they would get the 322 runs needed for victory. 'Imagine someone bowling a very hard projectile at you at 85 miles per hour and you don't know how it's going to behave off the pitch – that's a pretty scary prospect,' said Trego at the end of the second day. 'To be honest, I like wickets like that. It gets the juices flowing and there's the chance of a result. I'm sure their batsmen will scrap – they have quality players – but if we keep hammering away, I'm sure we will get our rewards.'

Yet what Trego had not considered was the gloomy English weather. Rain fell on Birmingham for the next 48 hours and the match was washed out. 'It was very disappointing,' said Rogers, who was also miffed about the pitch. 'On a wicket that was getting harder to bat on, we felt 320 was definitely a winning total. There were a few concerns about the pitch. The groundsman didn't quite get it the way he wanted to, though I think had a similar-looking wicket for their first game that didn't play anywhere near as badly. I have played on some excellent wickets here, so this was different.'

While they had gone four matches without a win, Somerset's performance at Edgbaston had indicated they were heading in the right direction. Rogers could see significant improvement in his young team. 'The innings from Tom Abell and Peter Trego were outstanding. They really gave us momentum and, particularly when you are playing a good side, if a couple of guys step up and lead from the front, it carries through the rest of the team. I think we bowled really well, pitched the ball up and challenged the batsmen and got our rewards.'

Somerset were beginning to compete in the Championship. Their final red-ball match before the start of the Twenty20 Blast was against Yorkshire at Taunton. The defending champions had become the team to beat in county cricket following their back-to-back titles, yet the hosts were not fazed. Batting first, Trescothick, Rogers and Trego all made significant scores but, frustratingly, all fell in the 90s. The only player to make three figures was Hildreth, whose score of 166 allowed them to declare on 562/7. They then hammered home their advantage. Despite a century from Adam Lyth, the attack – led by Groenewald's three-for – dismissed Yorkshire for 311 on the final day. Their lead was big enough to enforce the follow-on and they could push for victory. The champions, however, remained defiant. Alex Lees saw off 97 balls and Adil Rashid, facing 30 deliveries, made the best duck of his career as Yorkshire survived with four wickets in hand. 'That is the best we have played this season, so far,' said a pleased Rogers. 'On a very tough wicket to bowl on, we did fantastically well and nearly stole a win against the reigning champions. Let's face it, had it not been for the weather in the last two games, we would have probably won both matches.'

Despite their lack of victories, Somerset were beginning to grow in confidence under Rogers's leadership. It would not be long before they were winning Championship matches.

* * * * *

As well as aiming for a first Championship title, Somerset were also hoping to get back on track in white-ball cricket. They had struggled in recent years, but the permanent appointment of Allenby as captain marked the start of a new era for the team and he was keen to lead by example. In their first match of the Twenty20 Blast against Kent, Allenby opened and hit 91. But their score of 197/7 did not prove to be enough as Kent chased down their target with 16 balls remaining. It was a humbling defeat for Allenby's team, who had prepared well for the tournament. As well as having Allenby, van der Merwe and Trego in their squad, they had also acquired internationals Mahela

Jayawardene and Chris Gayle. At the time, the duo were the top two run scorers in the history of the World Twenty20. They were both huge coups. 'I really enjoyed my time at Somerset last year,' said Gayle, on returning for a second stint. 'It's a great club and the supporters were absolutely incredible.'

Somerset were expected to do well with such talent at their disposal, but they received another hammering in their second match. Sussex, thanks to Chris Nash's century and Luke Wright's 83, scored 222/3. Yasir Arafat, the former Pakistan bowler, endured a particularly tough day, conceding 47 off his four overs. He also struggled against Kent, conceding 48 off three overs. It was not a good start for Arafat, who had joined Somerset before the campaign. In reply they limped to a 48-run defeat as Gayle and Jayawardene struggled to match Nash's exploits. Gayle did manage to inspire them to victory in their third game against Essex – scoring 49 off 23 balls – but that was as good as it got. They finished bottom of the South Division, winning three and losing ten of their 14 matches. No team had a worse record in the tournament.

It was a challenging time for Allenby, who felt the pressure of captaining such a passionate club. 'It's certainly a different challenge, with the supporters being – passionate is probably the right word – about results,' admitted Allenby. 'The good days are really good, the bad days are really bad – you're either elated or think it's the end of the world. That is quite a challenge for a captain and a team. I'm sure that actually affects the team's performances, as well … Managing the emotions of the county and the supporters, and then subsequently the players, is a really big job when you're captaining Somerset.'

While Somerset's Twenty20 campaign was one to forget, there were some positives to take. Jamie Overton had a good tournament with the ball, taking 14 wickets at an average of 22.92, and Gregory proved himself to be a good all-rounder, scoring 196 runs and taking nine wickets. There was also the fact their young squad had another Twenty20 campaign under their belts. But there was not much else to celebrate. Somerset's Twenty20 plan had backfired.

* * * * *

Somerset's sixth Championship match of 2016 was a trip to Lord's. It was a venue Rogers knew well having spent four years at Middlesex, captaining them in 2014. He knew exactly how to bat at the Home of Cricket, scoring a handful of centuries there for Middlesex and hitting 173 for Australia during the 2015 Ashes series. So it was no surprise when he scored a century against his former club. He made 109, Hildreth hit 68 and Trego added 65 to help Somerset reach 376. In response the hosts showed no mercy. Openers Sam Robson and Nick Gubbins put on 198 for the first wicket in a dominant display. Gubbins reached three figures, but Robson was dismissed for 99. Somerset's attack fought back to reduce the hosts to 252/5, but that only brought Paul Stirling to the crease. The Irishman produced a stunning, counter-attacking 85 to get them to 423. As their innings closed on the fourth morning, the match was only going in one direction. Although Hildreth cashed in with an unbeaten 85, there was not enough time in the match to force a win and it finished with the visitors on 202/7.

Surrey were Somerset's next opponents in Division One. The London club were again blessed with the presence of

Sangakkara. This time, however, he was pegged back by Groenewald on 45 as the hosts consistently took wickets at Taunton. Steven Davies was dismissed on 49, Ansari was stopped on 37 and Ben Foakes was restricted to 31 as they were bowled out for 264. Leach, who took a five-for against Middlesex, again led the attack with four wickets. As Surrey's innings finished on the second morning, things were looking good for Somerset. But then came a woeful batting display. Having made their way to 73/3, they collapsed and were dismissed for 102. Batty tore through their lower order to finish with figures of 7-32. Leach had been upstaged by his experienced opposite number and Somerset were staring at a big defeat. If they were going to salvage anything from this match, they needed to dig deep.

And that is what they did. With Leach holding down an end, Craig Overton got to work. He dismissed Arun Harinath and claimed the big wicket of Sangakkara, who had added just three runs to the lead. Then Craig's brother Jamie came into the attack, taking four wickets. Leach also picked up a four-for as the visitors were bowled out for 138. Their lead was exactly 300, giving Somerset a slim chance of victory. And their chase started well. Despite Abell falling for seven, Trescothick steadied the ship. He went past 50 to get them up to 92/1 and give them more chance of winning the match. Yet Stuart Meaker turned the game back in Surrey's favour. He dismissed Trescothick and Hildreth in the same over. Rogers then fell shortly after to leave them on 127/4. But just as the match was starting to slip away from Somerset, Allenby and Trego put on 80 for the fifth wicket. When Trego fell for 44, Somerset had reached 207 and victory was now in sight. The match then swung back in Surrey's favour, however, as Allenby fell for

56 before another two batsmen were dismissed. They were now 237/8.

After performing with the ball, Jamie Overton confirmed his all-round abilities with a rapid 29 off 27 deliveries. He was supported at the other end by Leach, foreshadowing what he would produce during the Ashes Test at Headingley in 2019, when he, alongside Ben Stokes, put on 76 for the last wicket. When Overton fell with 31 still needed for victory, a Somerset win remained unlikely. Yet Groenewald proved just as defiant as Leach. The duo scored the required runs to seal a first Championship win of the summer at the seventh attempt. Somerset's fortunes were beginning to turn in their favour. 'Once we were eight down, I think I gave up, so I stopped being nervous and just sat down,' said Rogers after the match. 'But when we got to seven or eight runs to go, I got confident because Jack and Tim looked so good … It's definitely a turning point of the season. If we'd lost this game, I think we'd have been in the bottom two or three and now we've won it and we're up to fourth almost. So that's how easily it can turn around and it gives you belief. More than anything it makes you think you can win from any position.'

As it was their last game before a four-week Championship break, the result could not have come at a better time for Somerset. Their title challenge was alive.

* * * * *

June marked the start of the One-Day Cup. Somerset's Twenty20 campaign was going badly, so it was imperative they performed well in the 50-over tournament. Their first match was at Taunton against holders Gloucestershire, who were sent in to bat by Allenby. It was a wise decision as the visitors struggled to 260. The only man to score big was Chris Dent, who hit exactly 100 before Groenewald ended his innings. In reply a different-looking Somerset kept losing wickets. With Trescothick and Rogers no longer playing white-ball cricket, Myburgh and Adam Hose – a 23-year-old batsman – opened the batting. Myburgh played well, scoring 81 off 92 deliveries, but others struggled. Hose, Trego, Gregory, van der Merwe, Barrow and Craig Overton all fell cheaply to leave Somerset on the verge of defeat at 198/9.

But then, somehow, they managed to top their tenth-wicket exploits against Surrey in the Championship. Groenewald, this time joined by Jamie Overton, put on 65 to snatch the game away from Gloucestershire with just three balls remaining. It was another spectacular victory for Somerset. 'I think sharing a match-winning last-wicket stand against Surrey in our last Championship game gave me confidence that we could get the required runs,' admitted Groenewald. 'Jamie Overton played so well that it seemed easier than in the Surrey match. Both innings gave me an equal buzz … I just set out to bat properly and concentrate on each ball. The crowd were brilliant and we could really feel them behind us.'

As Groenewald said, the Taunton faithful are some of the most passionate and loyal cricket supporters in the country. The club is the main sporting attraction in this small, rural town and the locals turn up in their thousands for each match. Sometimes this can be difficult for players to handle, increasing the pressure on them. But they usually thrive, with the fans urging on every ball. It makes the County Ground a wonderful place to play cricket, as Michael Bates testifies. 'I absolutely loved it,' he said. 'I genuinely loved every minute at Somerset. The people there were brilliant, from the locals, the members and the public that come to watch cricket there. They absolutely love it; they live and breathe cricket. And all the blokes in the changing-room were incredibly down to earth, they were just really decent, sound people and they welcomed me with open arms.'

Victory against Gloucestershire was the perfect way to start the campaign. And things got only better. In their next match against Surrey, Myburgh continued his good form with 76 off 59 deliveries. There were also runs for Allenby, who made 71. Their efforts contributed significantly to an eight-wicket win in a rain-hit affair. There was more meteorological drama four days later as the Duckworth Lewis Stern method judged their close encounter with Essex to be a tie. In their final 50-over match before a six-week break, Somerset were bowled out for 136 as Kent recorded a huge win at Canterbury. That result, as well as the aggression they showed against Surrey, were examples of the way Allenby wanted to play. He wanted them to be positive, bold and exciting – a demanding philosophy that van Meekeren bought into.

'I really rate Jim,' said van Meekeren. 'I know he wasn't very much loved within the county, with the members, the fans and maybe some of the players, but I think he brought a bit of Australian culture – no bullshit, talking straight in your face. As a captain he took charge and said, "This is how we're going to play Twenty20 cricket in the powerplay, we're just going to go full blazing. If we get bowled out for 90 once or twice in the season that's fine. But in the other games we'll probably score 60 runs in the powerplay and that will set us up to win a lot of games." I always thought he was a very supportive captain and someone with a lot of experience. But the way he brought it across in the changing-room was something a lot of the guys didn't really appreciate. I think he was a fantastic player in the last few years he played for Somerset, as well. He performed with the bat and was a little bit underrated with the ball ... I could really get along with him and once or twice a year I have a quick catch-up with him. I liked his way of cricket; I liked the way he was thinking and you could always have a cricket conversation with him.'

While Allenby's positive approach had failed in the Twenty20 Blast and was perhaps responsible for the disappointing batting performance against Kent, they had made a decent start to their one-day campaign. Things were looking good for the white-ball side under his leadership.

* * * * *

Somerset's Championship campaign resumed with a trip to Southampton to face Hampshire. They endured a frustrating start to the match as Jimmy Adams batted well before Craig Overton dismissed him for 61. As they reached 184/3, it looked as if the hosts were going to post a big score. But then came a brilliant performance from Jamie Overton. He finished with 5-42 as Hampshire collapsed and were dismissed for 219. With Abell missing out through injury, Rogers took one for the team and opened the batting. Yet the move backfired when he was out for a golden duck. That brought Myburgh to the crease for his first Championship appearance of the summer. And he was far from rusty, scoring 110 alongside Hildreth, who hit 152. By the time Somerset declared on 474/8 with wicketkeeper Ryan Davies unbeaten on 52, they had a lead of 255. With

Hampshire 18/1 at the end of the second day, an away win looked likely. But the hosts played well in the second innings. Will Smith saw off 120 balls and 20-year-old Tom Alsop faced 101 deliveries as they finished the third day on 173/4. Rain then washed out the final day to deny Somerset back-to-back red-ball victories. They were now sixth in Division One, three points off second place, having played half their matches.

Although Somerset had been thwarted, it was a match to remember for Davies as he scored his maiden half-century in first-class cricket. After joining from Kent during the winter, the 19-year-old was not expected to play week in, week out. But he ended up becoming their first-choice wicketkeeper, playing 15 Championship matches in 2016. 'It was unbelievable,' said Davies, recalling the season. 'I'd come from Kent and only really played two or three Championship games up until that point. So I wouldn't have said I was guaranteed to have played when I came down … I think for the whole season I kept very well, but for the first half, batting wise, I was pretty awful. But towards the end it picked up and it was a very, very memorable year. And especially the players I was playing with. Tres, Chris Rogers, the Overtons, Lewis Gregory, Tim Groenewald. To get to play with Chris Gayle and Jayawardene and Jim Allenby – the list goes on. I was very, very lucky.'

The only Championship match Davies missed that summer was Somerset's next one against Middlesex at the County Ground. The visitors were the early pacesetters in the Championship, sitting one point clear at the top of the table. A defeat for Somerset would seriously harm their title hopes. After his heroics against Hampshire, Myburgh had been promoted to open, with Rogers reverting to his usual position. But it was Myburgh who suffered a duck on this occasion as James Fuller gave the visitors an early wicket. From there, they never really got hold of their innings. Although there was a decent knock from Rogers, who made a half-century, it was never going to be enough to post a big score. Their innings finished on 236. Middlesex then built a big lead as James Harris and Fuller put on 162 for the ninth wicket. From having them at 212/8, Somerset had allowed Middlesex to reach 381. It was a demoralising blow, but the hosts fought back. Trescothick and Trego both scored centuries as Rogers declared on 446/9 during the final morning, setting their opponents a target of 302 inside 46 overs.

With defeat unlikely and victory a real possibility, Somerset had pushed themselves into contention at the top of the table. But Middlesex had no intention of batting out a draw. From the very first delivery, they attacked. Malan made 32 off 28 deliveries and, crucially, Gubbins hit 76 off 70. Despite consistently losing wickets, Middlesex did not halt their chase. A powerful 36 off 18 balls from Fuller got them up to 271 and with one over remaining, they needed eight for victory. Rogers put his faith in Allenby's experience for the last, but he could not stop John Simpson. The wicketkeeper hit a six with two balls remaining to seal a remarkable victory and finish unbeaten on 79. Somerset had been confined to their first Championship defeat of the season. 'I am proud of our players,' said Maynard after the match. 'It was a fantastic game of cricket and we have come up just a bit short.'

The Middlesex defeat was cruel on Somerset – the type of result which defines a season. Knowing they could not afford to lose, Rogers gambled by declaring and it did not quite pay off. Many teams would fall apart after suffering such a brutal loss. They could have plummeted towards relegation with their Championship dream left in tatters. But the class of 2016, as had been shown in recent weeks, were made of sterner stuff. They used the result to start an assault on leaders Middlesex and defending champions Yorkshire, who were fighting for a third straight title. It began with a trip to Trent Bridge. Nottinghamshire were struggling in Division One and badly needed a victory. They started the match well as Steven Mullaney and Jake Libby shared a 196-run partnership. Somerset did claw their way back into the match thanks to four wickets from Craig Overton, but the damage had been done. The hosts had scored 401 to take charge.

But the wicket was flat, as was now proven by one of English cricket's great openers. Trescothick made 218, narrowly missing out on carrying his bat as the tenth wicket to fall. He was supported by his experienced colleagues Myburgh and Allenby, who both scored half-centuries. Their collective efforts had given Somerset a slim lead of 36. Their hopes were boosted by two late wickets during the third evening to leave Nottinghamshire on 58/2 and the game in the balance. But the visitors were not going to let this chance slip. They ran through Nottinghamshire to bowl them out for 135. Needing exactly 100 to win, Trescothick and Myburgh wasted no time in getting the required runs. They secured them inside 17 overs to seal an emphatic ten-wicket victory.

It was a massive result for Rogers, who was keen to highlight the importance of the Middlesex defeat. 'I read somewhere that I didn't have regrets about declaring,' said Rogers after the match. 'Of course I had regrets – we lost the game. It left us feeling low, but this group is going to get better by being in tough positions … We have a fantastic group of young players at Somerset for whom the sky's the limit and we have to challenge them. They responded so well to that loss and to see that response here, in one of the most incredible games I've played in, where losing the toss felt like a hammer blow, is so promising … This is a huge result, giving us a bit of breathing space and allowing us maybe to attack the teams ahead of us.'

One of those was Durham, their next opponents. The match at Taunton started in Durham's favour with Abell, on his return from injury, falling for a duck and Trescothick departing shortly after. Rogers, Hildreth and Craig Overton tried to wrestle back the initiative with decent knocks, but they could not cope with Durham's exceptional four-man seam attack of Chris Rushworth, Paul Coughlin, Graham Onions and Mark Wood. They were dismissed for 184 within 42 overs. Somerset's spinners, however, proved they could be just as prolific. Leach claimed five wickets and van der Merwe took four as Durham were bowled out for 189. With the visitors taking just a five-run lead into the second innings, it was game on. But Durham then seized the initiative as Trescothick, Abell and Rogers all fell without scoring. Somehow, the hosts found themselves three wickets down without adding any runs. The wickets kept tumbling and, with the score on 33/6, an embarrassing defeat seemed imminent.

But this was no ordinary Somerset team. Knocks of 47 from van der Merwe and 49 from Davies got them up to 180 and gave them something to defend. But with

Stoneman making 57 and Durham ending the second day on 130/5, it seemed as if they did not have enough runs on the board. Yet within the first 20 minutes of the following morning, Leach and van der Merwe had knocked over the tail and Durham were all out for 136. Remarkably, Somerset had won by 39 runs. 'I probably didn't see that happening overnight,' admitted an astonished Rogers. 'I thought we were in with an outside chance because the ball was turning and they had their tail end in. But it all went to plan ... To finish it that way is fantastic. All credit to the guys too, we were down and out on a couple of occasions in this game, but they fought.'

It was another resilient, brilliant performance from Somerset in this extraordinary Championship season. It was also a great individual display from van der Merwe, who showed his all-round ability with eight wickets and a crucial second innings knock. Steve Kirby, who played with van der Merwe at Somerset in 2011, appreciates how much of an asset he was to the club. 'Roelof, for me, was a standout character,' said Kirby. 'His energy, the things he used to do as an all-round cricketer. He was just great to have around the dressing-room.'

Another player who enjoyed playing with van der Merwe was van Meekeren, who also played with him at international level. 'I was lucky enough to get to know him in 2015 when he was playing in Amsterdam for ACC, which was my club at the time,' added van Meekeren. 'That year he got his Dutch passport and signed for Somerset for the 2016 season. With all the experience he brings in the white-ball game and the franchises that he's played with overseas, he's been one of the guys I've grown quite close to. I've spent time with his family and listened to what he's had to say about the game of cricket and bouncing my ideas, so he's definitely a standout player at Somerset.'

His performance against Durham proved just how important it was for Somerset to acquire van der Merwe's services on a full-time basis. It was a victory that saw them jump above Durham into second place, just three points behind Middlesex, who had drawn against Surrey. The title race was alive again and was getting tighter and more intriguing by the minute.

* * * * *

Somerset's One-Day Cup campaign resumed in late July with the visit of Glamorgan. Batting at No.4 was Jayawardene, who had joined the club primarily to play in the Twenty20 Blast. He made 37 on his one-day debut as Trego top-scored with 80. In reply Glamorgan failed to match Somerset's 322/7. They were bowled out for 279 as Craig Overton, Gregory and van der Merwe took three wickets each. That victory marked the start of a winning run. Middlesex were narrowly beaten in their next match with Trego scoring a century, they edged Surrey as Abell hit his maiden one-day ton and they defeated Hampshire thanks to some economical bowling from Max Waller and van der Merwe, each conceding fewer than 40 runs from their ten overs. The rub of the green had gone their way in those matches, ensuring they had finished top of the South Group.

That set up a home quarter-final against Worcestershire. Moeen Ali hit 81 off 76 balls to give Somerset a fright, yet there was not much else apart from that as the visitors were bowled out for 210. In reply the chasers eased to victory inside 37 overs. A match-winning 117 from Jayawardene secured a nine-wicket victory and a semi-final against Warwickshire, but it was unlikely he would be available for the tie. 'I think the semi is going to be tight,' he said in his post-match interview. 'I have already moved a few things around to play today, but prior commitments at home mean I have to go back now. Even this match was a bit of an extension, but I have had a great time here and if they get to the final, I might be able to make the trip.'

Without Jayawardene, Somerset struggled at Edgbaston. After Ian Bell's unbeaten 94 helped the hosts post 284/4, the chasers struggled to keep up with the pace. Jeetan Patel continued to take wickets, eventually finishing with a five-for, to derail their chase. Despite a late flourish from Groenewald, who made 30, they finished on 276/8 – eight runs short of Warwickshire's total. 'We thought 260, maybe 265, was a total we were looking at to chase but they had a really good over late on from Ian Bell,' Maynard told the press after the defeat. 'It is only the second game we have lost in the competition. It's just a shame it was the semi-final. We suffered a couple of decisions that didn't go our way but sometimes you get that.'

It was an agonising end to Somerset's indifferent white-ball season. While they had failed to perform in the Twenty20 Blast, their one-day exploits had suggested they were well on their way to becoming a force in white-ball cricket again. Their young stars, having been introduced in 2015, were flourishing under Allenby's positive captaincy – much to his delight. 'Although Twenty20 cricket went dreadfully that year, 50-over cricket was fantastic and once again we saw some of the younger players really stand up and come out of that tournament in a really positive way,' remembered Allenby. He remains proud that he helped

Somerset get closer to white-ball success during his time at the club.

* * * * *

Shortly before their semi-final defeat, Somerset welcomed Hampshire to Taunton. After winning the toss and electing to bat, the visitors began to slowly – but surely – tally up the runs. Former Zimbabwe batsman Sean Ervine scored 103 as they posted 338. It was a tough day and a half at the office for Leach, who bowled more than 40 overs. But he got his rewards, picking up six wickets. After seeing what Hampshire could do, the hosts began to pile on the runs. Abell hit 79 and Hildreth made 40. By the time Gregory fell for 61 with the score on 370/7, they were in the lead. Yet Rogers had no intention of declaring. He allowed both van der Merwe and Craig Overton, batting at No.8 and No.9, to complete centuries. When the latter fell at the start of the final day, Rogers halted the innings on 587/8 – a lead of 249. With victory no longer an option, Hampshire went for the draw. Although they lost Will Smith early on for a 12-ball duck, Adams and Ervine remained defiant. Adams lasted 268 balls on his way to 96 and Ervine hit his second century of the match. By the time Adams fell in the 90th over, the match was all but over. It finished with Hampshire on 254/5, comfortably securing a draw. It was a missed opportunity for Somerset, who perhaps should have gambled on the third day.

Their next match was a trip to Old Trafford to face Lancashire. After being put in to bat, the visitors made a big total. Abell carried on his good form by scoring 135 and Trego hit an unbeaten 154 off just 156 deliveries. 'I didn't go out there trying to chase boundaries, I just tried to watch the ball,' said Trego during the match. He was backed up by Davies's 86 as they put on a club-record eighth-wicket stand of 236. It was an effort that allowed Rogers to declare on 553/8, but that was as good as it got. Haseeb Hameed and Liam Livingstone hit half-centuries and a classy 155 from Alviro Petersen ensured Lancashire reached 422/9 at the end of the third evening. No play was then possible on the final day due to rain and Somerset were forced to settle for a draw. It was a huge blow to their title hopes as they remained in fourth place, the position they had slipped to after the Hampshire match.

And things got worse in their next game against Warwickshire at Taunton. After winning the toss and electing to bat, Somerset were bowled out for just 95. It was an embarrassing display with Trescothick, Rogers, Hildreth, Trego, Gregory, van der Merwe and Dom Bess – a 19-year-old spinner making his Championship debut – all failing to reach double figures. They had been humbled on home soil with their title dream hanging by a thread. But then came a Bess-inspired comeback. Not fazed by the magnitude of the occasion, he picked up six wickets to restrict Warwickshire to 123. It was an excellent display that had given them a glimmer of hope, yet they struggled to build on it. Although Rogers scored 58, they laboured to 211. They had set the visitors 184 to win, a tricky target on a spinning track.

The result, and Somerset's season, hung in the balance. But they rallied. Leach picked up five quick wickets to reduce Warwickshire to 61/8, seemingly winning the match. Warwickshire were not giving up without a fight, however. Rikki Clarke and Chris Wright put together a ninth-wicket partnership to edge them back into the game.

In the end it was Gregory's seam that did the trick. He had Wright caught behind for 45 before Leach finished off the job. Warwickshire were all out for 152, ensuring a 31-run victory for Somerset. It was a memorable win for Rogers, one which symbolised the talent and togetherness within the squad. 'We couldn't get this last wicket,' remembered Rogers. 'And I just turned to Lewy Gregory and thought, "He won't be able to do anything, it doesn't suit him." And he came on and just took a wicket. I just thought little moments like that where we did have such belief and such quality, all throughout the ranks that you could call on at different times, was fantastic.'

According to Allenby, much of their success was down to Rogers's influence. 'The great thing about county cricket is you play with international players, no matter where you are,' said Allenby. 'The Somerset players – Marcus Trescothick and James Hildreth and Peter Trego and these guys that will go down as club legends – it was great to play with them. Having played against Somerset for years, you thought the team was full of bravado and was quite a cocky and confident outfit. But after joining the club, I realised that confidence wasn't as deep as maybe I thought. And this is why Chris Rogers's captaincy was so important to getting the best out of a lot of guys.

'To have him as captain of one format while I was captain of the other, we were getting quite similar messages to the players, which I think was really helpful. We complemented each other; our values were quite similar and the players knew what to expect. We're both from Perth, so I'd known him since I was a kid. I knew he was very hard on his players, but not in a bad way, in a really good way. He expects a lot from you, especially the bowlers. I tried to let the bowlers know this. They were probably a bit surprised by how demanding he could be of them. But as we saw that year, they all got better because they knew the expectation was high and they had to meet that, otherwise they didn't get much of a bowl.

'I loved playing cricket with him because I find him fun. I think that sense of discipline and no excuses, which a lot of people talk about but rarely action. He was a 39-year-old man who had retired from international cricket, so he had nothing to lose. He could just lay it on the line and the way the guys responded was just fantastic. And that just showed how good of a season we had that year, having not had a great season before.'

Another player who enjoyed playing under Rogers was Davies. 'He brought a different style that I'd never known a captain to play with before,' added Davies. 'He wanted to play a certain way, but he wasn't very judgemental. He understood, and this was massive for me, that people were going to make mistakes. And he was very tolerant with them. He just wanted to help people get better. It wasn't so much about him at that point in his career, I don't think, because that was his last year. It was more about helping the younger guys to develop and that's probably the reason why he came back and coached the year after.'

Somerset's narrow win against Warwickshire had brought them back into contention with two matches to go. They were now up to second place, just two points behind Middlesex. Yet Yorkshire were still in the hunt, and after beating Durham a day later they leapfrogged Somerset ahead of their crunch clash at Headingley – a match the visitors had to win if they wanted to prove themselves as genuine title candidates. The game started in their favour.

Off the final ball of the opening over, Craig Overton had Alex Lees caught behind for a duck. From there, things only got better for Somerset. Although there were decent knocks from Jake Lehmann – son of former Australia batsman Darren – and Tim Bresnan, they bowled Yorkshire out for 145. Their batters then took centre stage with Trescothick, Rogers and Allenby all making half-centuries. Somerset's innings came to an end on 390 with Gregory unbeaten on 73. By the end of the second day, Lees, Gary Ballance and Andrew Gale had all been dismissed to leave Yorkshire on 57/3 and Somerset within touching distance of victory.

Although it was not an easy finish as Lehmann scored a century, Somerset always remained in charge. When Yorkshire's innings came to an end, Trescothick hammered an unbeaten 37 to help them knock off the 42 runs required and complete a crucial victory. It was another excellent effort from Leach, who now had 58 Championship wickets for the summer. His performance at Headingley is fondly remembered by Rogers, who described him as the stand-out player during that period. 'We set up games for him to be a force,' said Rogers. 'He was such an interesting guy, it's hard to describe Leachy. There was a time when he got something like six wickets in an innings. He came off and he was in tears because he'd got 6-100 when he thought he should have got 6-50. And he just felt like he'd let everyone down and we were like, "Mate, you've just got six wickets!" He was very much a team-first guy and people responded to that. He was just a force throughout the year. Of all the times I thought he'd bowled well it was that second innings against Yorkshire away. That was probably as good as any because it wasn't at home. He'd got six-for and it was just incredible bowling. He was flying at the time.'

Leach, in his first full season as the team's primary spinner, was beginning to show his potential to succeed at international level – something that his captain recognised. 'He had the game, even at that stage,' continued Rogers. 'There was this fierce, competitive spirit and he had great control. But there was still room for him to develop more to his game – more top-spin and more loop and things like that. You could just see it in him that he was prepared to really understand his whole craft, not just be a one-trick pony. Even the way he went about his batting and his fielding. He was desperate to improve in everything he did. The base was there, it was just whether he could handle some of the pressures. But I always felt that if I looked around, he could hold his own against any of the spinners in the land.'

Maynard added: 'He was not only accurate, but he spun the ball. If you've got those two attributes as a spin bowler you've got a great chance. What he worked hard on was driving through the crease a little bit stronger than he had been previously and therefore because of that, there was a little increase in pace without a lack of his drift or spin. And he became a proper threat and got used to handling the pressure of bowling in the fourth innings of the game when the wicket was spinning to get his result. I remember seeing Jack, I think, in 2010 when Glamorgan played Cardiff MCCU and thought that he had ability as a spin bowler but, at that stage, he was still very raw; he was a student at Cardiff. If anything, he was bowling a little too slow for first-class cricket, especially in the first innings of the match. But he learnt; he listened; he took things in and he's become a fantastic cricketer.'

Somerset's win had put them one point behind Yorkshire and just ten off leaders Middlesex. With their title rivals facing each other in the final match of the season, they needed to beat Nottinghamshire at Taunton and hope Middlesex and Yorkshire could not be separated at Lord's. If that scenario unfolded, they would, at long last, be champions of England. Somerset's match started well, despite the loss of Abell for eight. Hildreth and Rogers both hit centuries to put on 269 for the third wicket. It was a particularly impressive effort from Hildreth, who was struck on the ankle by a Jake Ball delivery. 'I quite enjoyed playing my shots and not having to run!' he joked at the end of play. When Rogers fell for 132, Somerset collapsed to 322/9, finishing the first day in a spot of bother. Yet it was still a good start to the match. 'It's frustrating,' Rogers told the press. 'I think to lose 7-20 from that position is pretty unforgivable to be honest and there were a couple of words said after the day's play. But we're still in a decent position and we just need to win the game now.'

Over at Lord's, Middlesex – the favourites for the title – had also made a good start. Gubbins had finished the day unbeaten on 120 as they reached 208/5. While it was not a huge total, it was enough to keep them in pole position. 'I don't know what's going on at Taunton,' Gubbins told the press after the day's play. 'Somerset have had a good day; it will be an interesting finish from what I hear. We can only focus on what we do. Whatever happens, happens – it's going to be a fun week of county cricket.'

As perfect days go, the second was as good as it gets for Bess. The spinner began with an excellent batting cameo, hitting 41 to help Somerset post 365. He then picked up a five-for to bowl Nottinghamshire out for 138. It was another spin-friendly pitch at Taunton, with Leach also taking three wickets. Somerset then reached 105/2 for a lead of 332. With clear blue skies ahead, a win looked likely. 'The last couple of weeks have been like a dream for me,' said Bess at the end of the day's play. 'To suddenly be involved in a team with a real chance of winning the County Championship has been fantastic. I really enjoy bowling in tandem with Jack Leach and he is always talking to me and offering advice.'

Over at Lord's, Yorkshire had clawed themselves back into contention. They pegged Middlesex back with the ball as their innings came to an end on 270. And despite Lees, Ballance and Gale all falling for ducks, they had reached 235/6 by the close of play. Yet the pressure was still on, as they had to reach 350 to gain an all-important batting point. If they did not, they could not win the title. 'With the clientele we've got in the dressing-room we never say never,' said a confident Bresnan, who was leading the charge on 72 not out. 'We've managed to win from some unbelievable positions this season and if we can get up to 350 we'll be in a good position.'

On the third day of this topsy-turvy race, Somerset made their mark. Davies hit 59 and Rogers made an unbeaten 100 to record twin centuries. A declaration came with his milestone as they had raced to 313/5. They then performed brilliantly with the ball, bowling Nottinghamshire out for 215. Somerset had won by 325 runs, meaning if the match between their title rivals ended in a draw, they would be champions. As they toasted victory in front of their adoring fans, Rogers delivered the news many had been expecting – his retirement from professional cricket. 'It's a pretty special way to go out,' said Rogers after the match. 'I remember Darren Lehmann being carried off at the Adelaide Oval after he had slogged 150 against us and I always hoped that

I could do something similar. But, not only that, we've had a fantastic year. To walk around and see the standing ovation from the Somerset supporters is a nice way to go out.'

He was not quite finished yet, however, as there was a good chance he would be lifting the Championship trophy 24 hours later. But not before an anxious wait. The match at Lord's was going right down to the wire as Yorkshire scored 390 thanks to Bresnan's unbeaten 142, meaning they could still win the title. In reply Middlesex were 81/2 as day three came to an end. It was impossible to predict which way this was going to go. 'We're a little bit confused up there as to the options and what we want to do,' said Middlesex's Tim Murtagh. 'We obviously want to win the game and try to win the title; that's a massive thing. But we don't want to just hand it to Yorkshire and set them something ridiculous. So who knows what might happen tomorrow?'

As play got under way at Lord's the next morning, the Somerset players collectively turned on one of the many televisions at the County Ground and began watching the deciding match, hoping it would end in a draw. The pleasant weather was doing them no favours, but there was still a chance. The day started well for Middlesex. Gubbins scored 93 and Malan made a century. Yet the runs were not flowing awfully quickly. If either side wanted to win, Yorkshire had to employ some declaration bowling. Lyth and Lees were brought into the attack, much to Somerset's horror, and were hammered for 128 runs off fewer than 12 overs. This allowed Middlesex to declare on 359/6, leaving Yorkshire needing 240 to win. But with only 40 overs remaining, they had to play aggressively. The title was slipping away from Somerset, who were utterly helpless. 'Both teams want to win, you can understand it, they're going to try and win at all costs,' said a dejected Trescothick. 'We're all pretty disappointed to see because it was heading in a certain direction, but let's wait and see.'

The start of the chase was tense. Runs were not being scored as freely as expected. At the halfway stage, 20 overs in, Yorkshire were 87/3. Both teams were still a million miles away from victory. But, just as belief was beginning to grow at Taunton, things started to happen. Ballance and Bresnan picked up the pace, which led to wickets. They fell for 30 and 55 respectively, leaving Yorkshire needing 83 off 54 balls and Middlesex requiring five wickets. With just nine overs of the season to go, it was still as unpredictable as ever. But Middlesex sensed victory. Gale was dismissed for 22, Azeem Rafiq was gone shortly after for four and, with just five overs remaining, Steven Patterson was bowled for two. Now Somerset's only hope was Yorkshire blocking out the remaining overs as there was little expectation the tail could get the 62 required.

And that was never going to happen. Two balls later, Toby Roland-Jones knocked over Andrew Hodd and Ryan Sidebottom to complete a stunning hat-trick and the most remarkable Championship finish in living memory. Somerset had missed out on the title by just 28 balls. 'We're all pretty gutted in the changing-room,' said Abell. 'We came so close. To have it taken away in the final moment of the season is very disappointing. At the start of the season we were written off a little bit. The end of the season probably came at the wrong time. It's a great advert for county cricket, what's happened over the last week or so and how it's unfolded.'

It was a horrible day for the squad, knowing they could do absolutely nothing to influence proceedings at

Lord's. It was perhaps hardest for the likes of Trescothick, Trego and Hildreth, those who had been through a similar experience six years earlier when Nottinghamshire pipped them to the title with minutes remaining in the season. 'It was an emotional, up-and-down roller coaster,' admitted Hildreth. Yet he and everyone else associated with the club could be proud of finishing second. Having endured a few apathetic seasons, they were back at the top end of the Championship and fighting for silverware again. And, considering the momentum they had gained, they could have been triumphant if the season had lasted just a little bit longer.

'We scrapped hard early on,' said Rogers, reflecting on the campaign. 'There was probably a little bit of me getting to know the players and the players getting to understand my style of captaincy ... And then we fought hard and we didn't really lose any games. The only game we lost all year was the one I took the gamble on against Middlesex. We found ourselves in really tough situations in the first half of the year, but we just managed to be able to get ourselves out of holes. And I thought it showed a lot of really good character because a lot of the time, to develop that kind of winning culture you've got to be prepared to try and stop losing almost. We won a couple of games and all of a sudden, we got on a fantastic roll. I reckon if the season would have gone on for one more game, we could have pipped it.'

As it was his last game in professional cricket, it was an emotional end for Rogers. 'There were so many mixed emotions going on,' he added. 'I knew it was my last game. I'd scored two hundreds – I got a single to bring up the hundred with the last ball I faced ... And then we ended up rolling Nottinghamshire easily and won by the end of that day. I can remember it all wrapping up really quickly and even the last wicket – I think I was at short fine leg, Leachy was bowling – and the ball went up in the air and I just thought, "That's it – I'll never play first-class cricket again." There were those emotions and then just seeing the crowd; there was such a big crowd for a domestic game and they were so behind us and so supportive. To win that game and do a little bit of a lap just felt so magnificent.

'And then, of course, that night we celebrated as if we'd won the title! I just think the feeling in the team, right at that moment, was absolutely brilliant. It was one of the few times in my career that I'd been part of a side that almost believed every time it walked out on to the field, it was going to win. And that's a pretty incredible thing to happen. I can share a few stories about that night, but I shouldn't!

'And then having to watch everything play out the next day. I could hear the crowd in the bar downstairs at Taunton cheering the Middlesex wickets and I just had this horrible feeling in my body thinking, "Oh no, I can see what's going to happen here and I think I know what's happened." Every time the crowd cheered, they didn't comprehend what was going down. And sure enough, it was almost kamikaze stuff and Middlesex came away with the win because the two sides had an agreement that Yorkshire would swing to the last. It was all a very bittersweet feeling throughout that last day because I was just so proud of how we played and even the role I'd had and my retirement. And we'd got so close but just couldn't get over the line.'

As Rogers says, he and his colleagues enjoyed quite the party after beating Nottinghamshire. Maynard had asked them to give Rogers the send-off he deserved and cap off an excellent campaign by celebrating as if they were Kings of England. 'We certainly celebrated that night,' joked Maynard. 'Obviously there was still one day to go in the season. Had it not been Middlesex and Yorkshire, I think there would have been a bit more from the ECB to be involved and make sure that a game wasn't set up so that Somerset didn't win it. As it transpired, both Yorkshire and Middlesex could win the Championship, so a declaration was given and obviously Middlesex succeeded with Toby Roland-Jones taking a hat-trick. But because it was those two sides, there was always going to be a result in that game, deep down. And that's why I asked the lads to celebrate properly in the dressing-room the night before, which we did as if we'd won it.

'But maybe in our hearts we knew it wasn't to be. We were leading it for a while, but we knew there had to be a result at Lord's. A lot of us were praying for rain in London! It was a near miss, but we can still be very proud of what we achieved that year having brought a good number of youngsters into that team. We'd lost the likes of Alfonso Thomas by that stage, so it was very much a young attack; young spinners … There were definitely some tough moments, it wasn't easy going. But I think the bigger thing is the players, prior to my arrival, appeared – and that's all I can say – to play individually. And when I left, they started to play as a team. We had a group of young players who enjoyed each other's success … We changed the psyche of the team.'

Davies added: 'I always think that our biggest downfall was that we won too early, in hindsight, because it gave Yorkshire and Middlesex an opportunity to set their game up. We were all watching it at the ground because we had the Sky cameras there and various players were doing interviews. Up until a certain point, everyone was thinking, "We're going to do this." They were playing on a flat track at Lord's, wasn't really giving much, and up until they declared everyone was very chipper. Saying that, even with ten overs to go I still think everyone thought, "This is ours." A lot of people had sore heads from the night before! We had a good night and it was a good day, it was just a shame of the outcome.'

For Somerset, it was indeed a shame. Considering the scenario that was unfolding at Lord's, they knew their chance of winning the title was slim. But when there is a chance, there is always hope that luck can go your way. In the end, it was not meant to be. Middlesex, the only team to beat Somerset in the Championship in 2016, deserved to be champions considering their unbeaten record. And ultimately that was the difference between the two sides. They both finished with six wins, but Middlesex were invincible. Yet the future was looking bright at Taunton. A new team was just emerging with seemingly unlimited time on their hands. An exciting era had just begun.

2018

Coming of Age

WITH CHRIS Rogers retiring, Somerset needed a new captain. To much surprise, the man to replace him was Tom Abell. The 22-year-old, who was announced as the new red-ball captain in December 2016, had just 32 first-class appearances to his name. It was a bold move by Matt Maynard considering Abell's age, experience and the fact he was succeeding two greats in Rogers and Trescothick. 'To follow on from some of the previous captains of the club who are listed on the honours board in the pavilion is an incredible feeling and something that I don't think will sink in for a while,' said Abell on his appointment.

While it was a brave decision, he was the obvious candidate because the squad backed him. 'I wouldn't say there was anyone else that would have done it, at that point,' said Ryan Davies. 'Yes, you had a lot of older players, someone like Hildy, but I don't think Hildy would have wanted to have done that. For me, it was between Lewis and Abes, really, and I think Abes was the perfect choice because you won't meet a nicer, better bloke and someone who loves the club as much as he does.'

Paul van Meekeren added: 'Tom becoming captain in 2017 was a bold move by the club. I think it's a move that will pay out in the future. He's a young, motivated guy. He's probably one of the hardest workers in the changing-room and one of those guys who is a leader, not only within the club but for cricket; the way he spends time doing community work and all that kind of stuff. I think looking at the way he's progressed in 2017, 2018 and 2019, you just see that he's learned to deal with the pressure that comes with those responsibilities. He has a very bright future in county cricket and if he keeps scoring some big runs, there will come an opportunity for England, I'm sure.'

Abell's personality and passion for the club is something many of his former team-mates pick up on. 'The player, for me, that stood out the most, as a young player, who is a fantastic human being as well as a cricketer, is Tom Abell,' said Steve Kirby. 'It's no surprise to me that he's now the captain and I think you'll see some very special things from that bloke. He will play for England and have a career for a long time … Everyone in the team just wants to play for him.'

Michael Bates, who played with Abell when he broke into the first team, added: 'Tom Abell is a brilliant bloke. Clearly a fantastic leader and it was a fairly ballsy call for Somerset to give him the club captaincy at the age he was. But clearly, they saw something in him – and rightly so. He's just learning and getting better and stronger as he goes. It was the same when I was there. Everyone is behind Tom, everyone loves him as a bloke, everyone respects him.'

The kind words offered by numerous former Somerset players proves how highly Abell is rated. Adam Dibble, who has been friends with Abell for years, knew he would become a top professional from a young age. 'I've known Tom since we were at Taunton School together,' said Dibble. 'I was his captain at school level when I was upper sixth and he was fourth form. I was in the academy and on the fringes of the squad and I knew that's what he wanted to do, so I think he asked a lot of me, in terms of looking at me and what I was doing; how I got myself a contract. He was able to apply that to his own game. He's a hell of a lot more talented than me and a better player.

'The *Cricketer's Who's Who* asked me my tip for the future and I put Tom Abell. I was young, so he would have still been at school. I could see then that as a player, there was no doubt about it that he was talented enough, technically brilliant and was going to go far. His main issue was his self-doubt and self-confidence. He was such a nervy character – always wanted to please everyone – and those nerves sometimes came in. Coming into the Somerset team he was so hard on him, which is a great attribute to have because you know he's always going to try and improve and get better. But it was becoming a little bit detrimental to his game. It made him tense up and not be the player we knew he could be.'

Dibble believes getting the captaincy helped Abell become a better player, much to Somerset's benefit. 'Being given the captaincy was the best thing for him,' he continued. 'It gave him that self-confidence to go on. As a captain, I don't know what he's like because he's never captained me. But I know he'll always listen to everyone, he'll take everyone's advice and I know, from when I speak to him year on year about this kind of thing, he's more confident in his decisions. When he first came in, it was a seriously daunting thing to do. Ultimately, and it sounds a bit harsh, but the captaincy was given to him because nobody else was available, really. He was the next best fit and, in most situations, he wouldn't have been given the captaincy at such a young age. But a little bit like Graeme Smith and South Africa – he was so young and look at what happened to him. Sometimes it takes these situations to get the best people in the right jobs.

'The thing about Abes is he leads from the front; he leads from his actions. He's a quiet guy, but people have so much respect for him because he just gets on with it. He's the hardest trainer; fittest bloke; nicest bloke, will always give people time. And when you've got all those attributes people will get behind you and fight with you. He won't have to speak that much and ask much of the guys, I'm sure. No doubt they're always behind him because they trust and have faith in him in the way he goes about his business. I'm the same age as his older brother and we all went to school together. Seeing him flourish is amazing – I'm so proud of him and he's doing a great job.'

Johann Myburgh, who saw Abell rise through the ranks at Somerset, also appreciates his qualities. 'He was very young, so he had a lot to learn,' said Myburgh. 'He's, in my opinion, a very good leader. I can't say great yet because he's still growing into it … He just leads as a human being and I think that's what you need at a club. I believe you're people first; you're humans first. And that impacts on your cricket and how you go about your business on the field. And Tom certainly leads by example, both on and off the field, in terms of the things you can control; in terms of the behaviour you want to show; in terms of the attitude you want to have.

'He cares a lot about his players and that shines through in the little things he does. It'll be difficult to sum up and tell you all the things he does but, for example, I'll use a very simple one. We've had a practice and there are cones lying around. Even though Tom Abell is the captain, he's the one who's collecting the cones and helping out. That's the type of guy he is. The standard he sets for the other guys, in terms of what is acceptable behaviour and what is an acceptable attitude, is high. But he lives by it, so it's easy for him to go to someone and say, "Listen, you're not quite getting it right." And he's got that touch about him as well. People are people and you're going to make mistakes … Sometimes you don't quite get it right and anything could have led to that. You might not have had any sleep; you might not be feeling great; you might have had some bad news. But you've got to front up as a sportsman and people don't always understand that there are human beings behind the sportsperson.'

There is no doubt Abell had the support of his team-mates and had all the qualities needed to become a great captain. But was he appointed too early in his career? To help him during his first season in charge, Rogers returned as a coach and Somerset signed wicketkeeper-batsman Steven Davies. The 30-year-old, who had made eight ODI and five Twenty20 appearances for England, had surrendered the gloves to Ben Foakes at Surrey and was desperate to force his way back into England's plans. 'I have made no secret of my desire to play for England again and I hope that a new challenge along with a return to wicketkeeping will help kick my career on to the next level,' said Davies. Dean Elgar was also signed as an overseas replacement for Rogers. The opener, who was part of South Africa's squad for their 2017 tour of England, was available for most of the season.

But apart from Davies and Elgar, Somerset did not make any huge renovations to their squad. Instead they decided to promote young batsmen Eddie Byrom and George Bartlett to their first team. It was another victory for the academy, but a huge gamble from Maynard – a gamble that did not pay off. Although they made it through to the quarter-finals in both the Twenty20 Blast and the One-Day Cup, Somerset struggled in red-ball cricket. Abell, now batting in the middle order, found it particularly tough. In his first four Championship innings, he scored only two runs. 'I wasn't performing at the start of the season,' admitted Abell in December 2017. 'I wasn't batting any differently, but you fail a couple of times and you start to question yourself and how you're playing.'

And things got only harder for Abell. After getting a pair in a day/night match against Hampshire in late June, he made the decision to drop himself from the side. 'I got a pair and was in tears on the bus,' he recalled. 'I realised at that point the time had come to drop myself. I was in a really bad place at that time. I couldn't see myself returning to form and it was gutting not to be able to fulfil the role I wanted to play as captain of the club. I was pretty disconsolate, but it was a decision which had to be made.'

But that decision said a lot about Abell's character – the fact that he was willing to put the team's interests first. Somerset were struggling at the wrong end of the table, just two points ahead of Warwickshire in bottom place. In their next match, with Abell watching, they recorded a crucial victory against Yorkshire at Scarborough. And when he came back into the team against Surrey, he made 96.

Although he was enduring one of the toughest times in his career, Abell was becoming a fine leader. It was the start of a revival for Somerset, who narrowly escaped relegation from Division One. Going into the final match of the season, ironically against Middlesex, they had to beat them to survive and send down their title rivals from 12 months earlier. And on this occasion, it was Somerset who were celebrating. The trio of Jack Leach, who claimed a five-for, Roelof van der Merwe and Dom Bess dismissed Middlesex for 113 on the final day of the summer to ensure survival by just a point.

The result did not come without its fair share of controversy, however. With Somerset's spinners taking 16 wickets, the amount of turn in the pitch at Taunton was subject to an investigation after Wayne Noon, an ECB cricket liaison officer, deemed it to be 'excessive'. The investigation could have led to a points deduction, which would have relegated Somerset. Yet it concluded that the pitch should keep its original 'below average' mark, meaning they would not face such a penalty. But they were still not out of the woods. Middlesex had unofficially appealed against a two-point deduction for a slow over-rate, which came during their match against Surrey. The match was bizarrely abandoned after an arrow fired from outside the ground landed on the field. A week or so later, their penalty came. 'All the information we had when we left the ground was that we were not going to lose the points,' said Middlesex director of cricket Angus Fraser. 'To suddenly find out that we do further down the line is pretty gut-wrenching.'

Much to the relief of Somerset, who were threatening legal action if the decision was reversed, Middlesex's penalty was upheld. Abell was pleased after a challenging year for him. He had grown immeasurably as both a player and a leader. 'It's far and away the best day of my career,' said Abell after Somerset secured their safety. 'I have been through some pretty dark times as captain this season, so to finish on such a high note is a very special feeling … From where we were four games ago, it has been a terrific effort by the team and I am very proud of all the players. The future here is bright and there is a lot to look forward to. My overriding feeling is one of elation.'

Rogers, who questioned the appointment of Abell at the time, recognises how important that first year was. 'If I'm being honest, at the time I probably didn't feel it was the right decision,' admitted Rogers. 'I just felt that it would have been so much pressure on Tommy to have to carry that. But in hindsight, I think it was the right decision and I give Matty Maynard a lot of credit for that – that he had enough faith in Tom to do that. Now that I'm in coaching and I understand a little bit more, you want that person who really drives the standards and drives other people to want to be better – and that was Tommy. There's not a person who says a bad word about Tommy Abell. He's the guy who's first at training; he's the last one to leave. He throws balls at other people. He's just that guy who has real leadership qualities.'

Maynard had recognised that any potential short-term stress was worth it for the long-term future of the club. But while he can now take a huge amount of credit for appointing Abell, at the time it played a part in him losing his job at the end of 2017. Jim Allenby recognises the strain that season caused. 'If I'm honest, it was the wrong decision,' said Allenby. 'To put the club under the pressure that it was put under halfway through the season – being bottom of the division having nearly won it [the season before] – was, personally, quite challenging to sit and watch that and not get a game. I don't really know the kind of captain he was. I know he's a little bit more emotional, probably, than Chris. It's his club and it means the world to him and it's the most important thing in his life, so his heart and soul went into it. Whether he was able to emotionally deal with the challenges of captaining a big club with high expectations, I'm not sure.'

Maynard, however, has no regrets and highlights how big of a loss Rogers was. 'He was instrumental, there's no doubt,' said Maynard while discussing Rogers. 'His leadership qualities, how he managed the players on the field, was very important. He spoke to me with about four games to go to say that he'd had enough; he'd found it tough batting at times; he had flashbacks to what happened to Phil Hughes; he felt he'd lost his nerve a bit. But I knew he was essential to us. I managed to convince him to just enjoy it, don't worry too much about whether he gets nought or 50 or 30, but just to go out and enjoy the game for the last four or five games of his career and take it in. And thankfully he did that and he had a wonderful finish by scoring two hundreds in the match against Nottingham. Obviously he was going to step down at the end of that year. It was sad because it was always going to be a two-year plan with Chris. But almost that love of the game had gone for him and he wanted to go on to the coaching side.

'We missed him dreadfully in what turned out to be my last season in 2017. But it allowed a very promising young captain and player in Tom Abell to take the helm … Tom has gone on to prove himself as a really good and capable leader of men and that's been brilliant to see. We could have gone for a more conservative route. But I've never been one just to look at what I need – at that stage I didn't know that I was going to lose my job at the end of the year – and [it was a question of] what is best for Somerset in the medium and long term? And that was Tom Abell to take the reins. I had absolute belief in his ability as a leader and obviously as a high-class player ... I've got no regrets whatsoever. Had we been relegated, then I probably would have had because I would have felt like I'd put too much on young Tom's shoulders. But we didn't and the toughness of that year will have helped develop his skills as a leader, as well. He came through it. He doubted himself a couple of times, but now I assume that he will have really enjoyed that experience as something that motivated him to be as good a captain as he is now.'

Somerset had survived 2017 without any lasting damage. But with Maynard gone, they needed a new director of cricket. The man who got the job was Andy Hurry, an old favourite at the County Ground. After coaching them to the Division Two title in 2007 and playing a huge role in their revival, he returned to take the top job. 'Somerset will always hold a very special place in my heart and it's an honour to once again be associated with the club,' said Hurry on his appointment. 'There is some unfinished business. It feels very much like I'm coming home.'

There was also a promotion for former academy director Jason Kerr, who became the new head coach. It was the first time Kerr had been appointed to such a position in his career, yet he did not change his approach to coaching. 'Ultimately you want to be successful,' said Kerr. 'And I guess it's the definition of success that's important. Yes, we want to win trophies; it's well documented the Holy Grail of never winning the County Championship. So certainly you've got aims to be successful from a silverware point of view, but I think it's really important as well that you're very aware of what the individual's aspirations are. So it's about producing international cricketers; it's about playing a brand of cricket that people want to watch. And trying to develop people as well. A huge part of my philosophy is relationships and helping people on their journey. We're all passing through this great club and it's about having as big of an impact as you can on as many people, while you've got the opportunity to do that. So I was really excited by the opportunity for lots of different reasons.'

And it is not just about developing players. Kerr wants everyone at the club to grow as individuals and fight for a common goal. 'Everyone plays a huge part, it's part of our values as a club,' he continued. 'There's a real family feel there. And for me it's actually trying, through the medium of cricket, to bring everyone into that family; making sure the people on the gate are as passionate and interested and supportive of what we're trying to achieve on the field. And they feel they're contributing – because they are. Someone's experience of coming to watch us could be really important to whether they return and watch again … We've got a wider responsibility.'

Hurry's first decision was to retain Abell as captain. Having learned so much from the last 12 months, he was willing to stick with him. Not only that, but he had been given a promotion. Following the departure of Allenby, he was made one-day captain, with Lewis Gregory getting the Twenty20 job. Hurry had total confidence that Abell was the man to lead the club forward. 'Tom is an outstanding young man,' said Hurry following Abell's appointment as one-day captain. 'There was never any doubt in my mind that he would captain the side again in 2018. He is a real leader both on and off the field and he epitomises everything about the culture that we have created here. In a bid to retain a certain degree of consistency we also feel that both Tom and the club will benefit from him captaining in the One-Day Cup as well.'

There was never any hesitation in Kerr's mind either that Abell should remain as captain. 'I was heavily involved in the process of Tom being announced as captain initially,' said Kerr. 'For me, it's a no-brainer. Leadership is incredibly important, whether that's from myself, the captain, the players or the hierarchy at the club. You need strong people; you need people that people are going to follow, ultimately. And Abes demonstrates so many good qualities. He's starting to now show how good of a player he is on a regular basis and I think his future is incredibly exciting. Our relationship is strong and I love the challenge of working with him, making sure he's growing on a daily basis and that actually he's going to fulfil his potential as a cricketer and a leader.'

Gregory's appointment was also a glowing reference of his development during the last few years. Although he had suffered with a back injury during the previous two seasons, he had been a consistent bowler since he became an important member of the first team in 2014, picking up nearly 150 first-class wickets. 'Lewis has established himself as a key member of the squad with the bat, the ball and within the dressing-room,' said Hurry on Gregory's appointment. 'His journey thus far has demonstrated that he has the potential to evolve into a great leader.'

The next big decision was whether to stick with the youngsters. After seeing how much the team struggled in 2017, this was a huge call. They decided to be brave and not bring in any senior professionals during the winter. They still had Peter Trego, James Hildreth and Trescothick on the books, however, with the latter now 42. 'My hunger, desire and passion to play is as strong as it was when I started,' said Trescothick as he entered his 26th year as a professional. 'The club itself, along with the members and supporters, have stuck by me through thick and thin and it's an honour to step out into the middle and represent them.'

The reason why Hurry decided not to make any major signings was because he was a huge fan of the talent already in place. 'I'm quite switched on by the fact that I can see the potential at this club,' said Hurry. 'A great mix of youth and experience. And we've got some great people here. I knew it didn't need much from me, they just needed to ensure they were all going in the same direction with a clear strategy. It was my opportunity just to check and challenge and just nudge a couple of areas. But it's under the leadership of the head coach Jason Kerr and the captains Tom Abell and Lewis Gregory. Their maturity and development have allowed the club to kick on again in the last couple of years. I haven't really done that much … We've worked well together, collaboratively, to make sure we know the things that are important to this club. We develop our own players; we provide opportunities in first-team cricket; we develop people, whether that's coaches or players. And that ethos has served us really well.'

Although Somerset had no intention of bringing in an experienced county professional, they did sign an overseas player. Cameron Bancroft, who was opening the batting for Australia in the Ashes as his signing was announced in December 2017, was set to follow in the footsteps of his compatriots Langer and Rogers. 'This will be a key ingredient to us achieving our aspirations of winning silverware,' said a confident Hurry on signing him. But Bancroft, who said he was 'really excited to be joining a county with so much potential', never got the chance to represent Somerset. Just a few months later, he was involved in the ball-tampering scandal that rocked Australian cricket. In a plan devised by his captain Steve Smith and vice-captain David Warner, Bancroft used sandpaper to alter the condition of the ball during a Test match against South Africa. He was handed a nine-month ban by Cricket Australia for his actions and had his Somerset contract cancelled.

They replaced him with another Australian, Matt Renshaw. The 22-year-old, who was born in Yorkshire, had been capped at Test level and was a promising talent. 'I've heard a lot of good things about the club and I understand that I will be following in the footsteps of some outstanding Australian batsmen,' said Renshaw. Although he was talented, Renshaw was another youngster in an inexperienced squad. With Somerset putting their faith in youth again, they were expected to struggle. *Wisden Cricket Monthly* and *The Guardian* both predicted relegation and *The Cricketer* envisaged a sixth-place finish. Yet they were a year older, a year wiser. Abell and his colleagues had learned from one of the toughest summers of their short careers and were determined to show what they were capable of. It was all set to be an intriguing season.

* * * * *

Somerset's Championship campaign began with the visit of Worcestershire, who had won Division Two the previous year. Batting at No.3, it was not long before Renshaw was called upon on his debut. After Trescothick fell for one inside four overs, he came to the crease and produced a masterclass. He hit an unbeaten 101 to guide Somerset to just 202, saving his new colleagues after some dire batting. But as they say, you should never judge a match until both teams have batted. The visitors were bowled out for 179 thanks to four wickets from Gregory. It was a similar story in Somerset's second innings, only this time it was Hildreth who held it together. Now 33 and into his 16th Championship season, he made an unbeaten 111 to remind the England selectors of his effortless talent. It was a knock that helped Somerset reach 255 and a lead of 278, a match-winning total if the previous three innings were anything to go by. In the end, it was a comfortable 83-run win for the hosts. It was the perfect start to their red-ball campaign. 'We are delighted to get off to a winning start,' said Gregory.

The performance of Somerset's four-man seam attack – Craig Overton, Josh Davey, Tim Groenewald and Gregory – had done the trick against Worcestershire with 19 wickets. Although they are renowned for producing quality spinners in George Dockrell, Leach and Bess, Somerset have had some excellent seamers in recent years. At the beginning of the decade, they had Kirby, Charl Willoughby and Alfonso Thomas. And in 2018 they had similar quality, but also depth. Along with the four who played against Worcestershire, they had Jamie Overton, van Meekeren and Abell in reserve. This was tough for van Meekeren, who found it difficult breaking into the first team. 'I've played there and no one can take that away from me,' he remembered. 'I would have liked to have played more games, but with the bowling attack we've had with the Overtons, Lewis Gregory – Tom Abell has shown over and over again how good of a bowler he actually is. And then you've got guys like Josh Davey and Tim Groenewald. It was very tough to get into the first team.'

This competitiveness was excellent news for Hurry, who wanted to see quality players such as van Meekeren pushing the likes of Groenewald and Davey to improve. The win against Worcestershire was followed by the visit of Yorkshire, a match which started frustratingly as rain washed out the first day. When play did begin, Renshaw delivered another superb performance. The Australian hit 112 off just 99 balls to help the hosts reach 216. The quality of the innings was amplified by Yorkshire's poor effort, as they were bowled out for 96. Again, it was the seamers who got the job done, with Gregory and Tim Groenewald sharing six wickets. 'Matt Renshaw has come out and played like it was a Twenty20 game for them,' said Yorkshire coach Andrew Gale. 'I can't remember seeing a Championship innings in April like it.'

More wickets followed throughout the next day as Somerset struggled to build partnerships. There was a good performance from Jack Brooks, who took his tally in the match to eight wickets – a solid audition for a man who would soon be calling the County Ground his home. The hosts were only saved by Abell's 82, an innings which got them up to 200 and a lead of 320. Yorkshire proved incapable of chasing down the total and were bowled out for 202, the seamers sharing the wickets. Somerset had made the most of the April conditions to secure two big wins.

'The magic wand behind winning our first two games is all the hard work put in by the players and the coaching staff during the winter,' Hurry told the press. 'It was a tougher game than our first win over Worcestershire and it took a real team effort to come out on top.'

Batting conditions were much more favourable in Somerset's next match at Old Trafford. After winning the toss, Abell elected to bat and was unfortunate to be given out lbw on 99, a brave call by the umpire. Yet Trescothick and Bartlett did make centuries as they scored 429. Their lead was reduced by Lancashire, however, along with their hopes of winning the match. Keaton Jennings scored 109 and Dane Vilas made an unbeaten 235 as they reached 492. It was not all bad news for Abell, who picked up four wickets, but that was as good as it got. An important 66 from Leach meant the match faded into a draw with Somerset closing on 269/8. 'We were a little bit twitchy there at a few stages,' admitted Abell afterwards. 'It was a tough four days of cricket and we had to work really hard. From the position we had during the first innings we were a bit disappointed to finish in the manner we did … But I have to pay tribute to Jack Leach. We've asked for character and fight, so to see him step up in the way he did was fantastic.'

And the result was not the only thing that frustrated Somerset. Trescothick had suffered a broken foot and required surgery. He would not play again for the first team until July. 'There are much worse things in life than a broken foot,' said Trescothick. 'I'll definitely still be hanging around the place. I'll certainly be trying to help out the other lads as much as I can.'

Somerset's final first-class match before a four-week white-ball break was against Hampshire at Taunton. After winning the toss and choosing to field, the hosts took charge. Three wickets from both Groenewald and Abell stopped Hampshire building any substantial partnerships and they were dismissed for 231. Somerset then built a big lead. A classy 184 from Hildreth was supported by some excellent knocks, including a useful 80 from Craig Overton. At No.10, Bess almost scored his second first-class century, but he fell eight runs short. Nevertheless, his effort had helped them post 506. A win was now in sight, but then came a vintage innings from one of English cricket's most elegant batsmen. James Vince, batting alongside the great Hashim Amla, made an unbeaten 201 to secure a draw for Hampshire.

Somerset were hampered in their efforts by the loss of Leach. While facing Kerr and his dog-ball thrower in the nets, Leach broke his thumb. He missed Vince's performance and in hindsight, they missed his international quality. 'Unfortunately, I have to take responsibility for Jack's injury,' said an apologetic Kerr. 'He will probably be out for around six weeks. I think I am more distraught about it than Jack. It is wretched timing when he was probably about to be selected by England again, but I know he will work hard and there is plenty of Test cricket later in the year.'

Leach was replaced in the England squad by Bess, who impressed against Pakistan with a half-century at Lord's and three wickets at Headingley. Although Leach would have been gutted to have missed out on playing Test cricket, he was not dearly missed by Somerset as he had become a red-ball specialist. As they began their one-day campaign, Leach's job was to get fit and ready for the resumption of Championship cricket in June. All eyes were now on the One-Day Cup.

* * * * *

Somerset's white-ball campaign began with a successful trip to the Oval. They dismissed Surrey for 129 before completing an eight-wicket win. It was another impressive display from Craig Overton, who was now an England international having made his Test debut during their 4-0 defeat to Australia in the 2017/18 Ashes. He picked up four wickets before Johann Myburgh blasted them to victory with an unbeaten 75. They followed that up with another convincing victory, this time against Glamorgan at Taunton thanks to a career-best score of 159 from Hildreth. 'As the sun got on it, it turned into a wicket on which runs could be scored freely,' said Hildreth afterwards. Making just his second one-day appearance was Tom Banton, a young wicketkeeper-batsman. The 19-year-old had enjoyed a rise to prominence since making his Twenty20 debut the previous summer against Middlesex. Batting at No.3 for England in the 2018 Under-19 World Cup, he scored a century to flaunt his talent on the international stage. But against Glamorgan he had an innings to forget as the leg-spin of Colin Ingram dismissed him for 11. And it was not a great day for Abell either as he fractured a finger. It was an injury which ended his one-day campaign – a tough start to the captaincy.

Banton struggled again in the next match and so did his team-mates. He scored just two as Sussex inflicted a 75-run defeat at Taunton, although he did score 40 against Essex as they lost again. Somerset got back to winning ways against Middlesex, but a 28-run defeat against Kent and a washout against Gloucestershire left them in a precarious position. To qualify for the knockout stages, they needed to beat Hampshire in their final match and hope results elsewhere went their way. 'We've been a little bit hot and cold in this competition,' admitted Abell. 'We've seen the best of ourselves, but in other games we haven't been up to the mark. It's been slightly frustrating, but it's a tough competition full of good sides, who will beat you if you're not at the races. Tomorrow is a massive game. I'm confident that on our day we can beat anyone, we just need that consistency.'

They did beat Hampshire thanks to a vintage century from Trego, but it was not enough. Other results did not fall in their favour and they finished fourth in the South Division as Hampshire went on to win the tournament. Their one-day campaign had lasted just eight matches.

* * * * *

Somerset's first Championship match following the break was against Nottinghamshire at Taunton. Abell was fit again but Leach's thumb had not recovered in time, so Bess was picked. He was not required to bowl on the first day, however, as they batted well. A century from Renshaw, 57 from Abell and an unbeaten 59 from Steve Davies, now the only Davies in the squad following Ryan's departure, helped them reach 307/7 at the end of the opening day. Davies was not able to reach his century the next morning as they were bowled out for 392, leaving him stranded on 92 not out. Nottinghamshire were then bowled out for 134, a total that could have been even lower had it not been for New Zealand international Ross Taylor, who hit 74. Yet they fought back after Abell enforced the follow-on. Half-centuries from Steven Mullaney, Chris Nash, Samit Patel and a century from Tom Moores helped them post 505.

Abell's declaration looked to have backfired, but the fact Nottinghamshire had scored such a big total suggested it was a good pitch. And so it showed as Somerset chased 248. Renshaw made 61 and Bartlett hit 43 before an unbeaten 87-run partnership between Abell and Davies finished the job. It was a win that moved them up to first in the table. 'It's a great feeling being top of the Championship, but there is so much more cricket to be played and so much more work for us to do,' said Abell. 'We are just concentrating on improving as a side with every game. It takes such a lot to win four-day matches. Every player has stood up in this one to earn us another win. Now the next fixture against Surrey becomes massive. I honestly believe we have a strong enough squad to beat any team in the country.'

As Abell suggested, the match against Surrey was the biggest of the season. The London club, who had just beaten Hampshire by an innings and 58 runs, were in ominous form. Placed just behind Somerset in second, they had excellent batsmen in captain Rory Burns and promising youngster Ollie Pope. And their attack, led by former South Africa seamer Morne Morkel – a man with more than 500 international wickets to his name – was equally good. A victory at Woodbridge Road in Guildford would be a monumental result for Somerset. They made a poor start to the match, however. Burns opened with 66 and Pope gave the England selectors something to think about with an excellent 117 at No.6. Pope was called up to the Test squad just two months later, with his skipper following a few months after that. Their efforts had allowed Surrey to post 459, putting them firmly in control. It was a particularly tough innings for the returning Leach, who went wicket-less.

Somerset's response started well, with Renshaw and Byrom putting on 53 for the first wicket. But when Renshaw fell on 39 to Rikki Clarke, they slipped to 63/3. Byrom managed to go past 50 as he held the innings together, but his dismissal two runs after reaching his half-century triggered a collapse. Having been 169/4, Somerset were bowled out for 180, with Leach suffering a nasty bout of concussion. It was a nightmare for the visitors, manufactured by medium-pacer Ryan Patel, who finished with career-best figures of 6-5. He bowled fewer than four overs. 'It's all a bit surreal to be honest, I can hardly believe what's happened,' said Patel at the end of the second day. Somerset were forced to follow on – and they did not fare much better in the second innings. Apart from an unbeaten 89 from Hildreth, there was little resistance as Morkel worked his magic. He picked up a four-for, as did former England bowler Jade Dernbach, to bowl them out for 210. Surrey had won by an innings and 69 runs to go top of the Championship. It was a convincing defeat for Somerset. 'It's obviously disappointing,' said a dejected Hildreth. 'Probably down to a mixture of bad batting by us and some good bowling by Surrey … We will just have to regroup and get back to it against Essex on Monday.'

Somerset were now playing catch-up with their title rivals and, as they travelled to Chelmsford to face the defending champions, it did not get any easier. Essex openers Nick Browne and Alastair Cook put on 151 for the first wicket. And their lead only grew after Browne was dismissed while backing up on 66. Centuries from Ravi Bopara and captain Ryan ten Doeschate allowed the latter to declare unbeaten on 517/5. Back-to-back defeats were now a real possibility for Somerset, but they rallied. Half-centuries from Byrom and Hildreth were the standout performances in a team effort. Eight batsmen managed to score 30 or more as they were dismissed for 407, cutting Essex's lead down to 110. Eyeing up a win, the hosts went on the offensive. Bopara's 58 and Simon Harmer's 30 off 27 balls helped them reach 208/7, a lead of 318. Their skipper declared for the second time in the match, tempting Somerset to attack and go for the win. And his plan almost worked. Essex picked up five wickets inside 20 overs to leave their opponents on 116/5. At this point, Abell decided to bat out a draw. He and Gregory, his reliable deputy, saw off the remaining 29 overs to deny Essex. 'The situation dictated how we played a little bit,' said Abell. 'We were looking to be very positive and had the intention to chase down the target … They put us under a lot of pressure, but I'm proud of the way we fought.'

Yet Abell's pride could not make up for his disappointment at results elsewhere. Surrey had beaten Yorkshire by seven wickets at Scarborough to move 32 points clear at the top. With so many international players in good form, the Londoners were beginning to look unstoppable in red-ball cricket. Things had changed very quickly at the business end of the Championship and Somerset's title hopes were beginning to fade.

* * * * *

While Somerset's Championship campaign hung in the balance, they still had every chance of winning silverware in the Twenty20 Blast. They had recruited well for the tournament, re-signing big-hitting New Zealander Corey Anderson, who had played for them the previous summer during an injury-hit spell. 'I feel I have unfinished business and I hope I can help Somerset go all the way in 2018,' said Anderson on his return. He was joined at the County Ground by West Indies seamer Jerome Taylor, who had plenty of experience of playing in the Indian Premier League and the Caribbean Premier League. 'It's a real honour to join such a prestigious club and I hope that I can help bring my experience to what looks like a really exciting group of young players,' said Taylor. The duo had added some much-needed international quality to a young squad.

Somerset's Twenty20 campaign began with a home match against Gloucestershire. Under new captain Gregory, they won comfortably. Davies, opening the batting, hit 60 and Trego made an unbeaten 72 to seal a six-wicket win inside 17 overs. They got a taste of their own medicine in their next match, however, as Kent won at Taunton with more than three overs to spare. Then Gloucestershire had their revenge, beating Somerset with five balls remaining in Bristol in a match reduced to 11 overs a side. It was not the start Gregory was looking for, but things got better. They won a further nine matches to secure top spot in the South Division. There were some big individual performances on the way. Jamie Overton, who had played only one Championship match all year before the tournament began, picked up 4-24 against Surrey and 3-23 against Essex. Taylor was also impressive throughout, picking up 22 wickets and a five-for against Hampshire.

And there was Myburgh, who scored an unbeaten 103 off 44 balls during a ten-wicket win against Essex. His opening partner that day was Banton, who showed glimpses of his talent with an unbeaten 29. It was a joy for Phil Lewis to see another youngster from King's College become a professional cricketer. 'He was very good at the basics, even though he had all the shots,' said Lewis. 'For Tom it was about training him to become a little bit more professional about how he dealt with situations. But also how he trained and that sort of thing, really trying to build the foundations for when he leaves school and becomes a professional. And I think that set him in a really good place as soon as he left because he not only had the game plan, but he also had the ability to confidently break into the top-flight team and back himself to be there.'

The Twenty20 Blast had been a tournament to remember for Somerset. Their finish at the top of the South Division had guaranteed them a home quarter-final against Nottinghamshire. Not only were they the defending champions, but they had also beaten Somerset at this stage in 2017. Yet there were no nerves at Taunton as the hosts completely blew away their opponents. A quick 52 off 28 deliveries from Hildreth set them on their way before Abell and Gregory hit unbeaten knocks of 46 and 60 respectively to post 209/5. Even with the quality of Alex Hales and Dan Christian, Nottinghamshire could not catch them. They were bowled out for 190 as Somerset progressed to Finals Day. It was another excellent performance by Jamie Overton, who was delighted to reach the semi-finals. 'We haven't been to Finals Day for a few years, so it will be nice for me to get there and see what the atmosphere is all about,' said the seamer after the match. 'We beat Sussex at Hove recently so we go there with a positive attitude and hopefully we can put one over them again.'

Somerset were heading to Edgbaston for their first Finals Day in six years. After qualifying for the big day four years in a row between 2009 and 2012, it had been tough for them to miss out. But under Gregory's captaincy, they had become a force in Twenty20 cricket again. With Finals

Day just on the horizon and a Championship title still to fight for, there were plenty of things for Somerset fans to get excited about as the season reached the home straight.

* * * * *

Between 25 June and 19 August, Somerset played just one Championship match due to the prioritisation of limited-overs cricket. It was against Worcestershire at New Road and Abell had lost one of his best players. Renshaw's time at Taunton was over after he suffered a broken finger in their defeat against Surrey. 'It's a huge blow to us because he has been brilliant both on and off the field,' said Kerr. Replacing him was the Pakistan batsman Azhar Ali. The 33-year-old, who had 14 Test centuries to his name, was an ideal substitute for Renshaw. He was a quality batsman and, having captained his country, offered priceless leadership on the field. He also knew what it was like to bat at the County Ground having made a century there during a tour match two years earlier. 'The standard of first-class cricket in England is very high and I hope that I can make a contribution to Somerset winning matches,' he said. 'I have heard good things about Somerset and I was impressed by what I saw at Taunton in 2016.'

Azhar was called upon early on debut as Byrom and Trescothick, making his comeback from injury, fell cheaply. His 27 steadied the innings before half-centuries from Hildreth, Abell and Davies helped them post a decent first innings score of 337. In reply Worcestershire struggled to deal with Jamie Overton. The seamer, who was bowling beautifully in the Twenty20 Blast, picked up four wickets as they slipped to 257. Davey also picked up a four-for. The visitors then began to build a big advantage. Trescothick scored a much-needed 71 to regain some form, and Azhar hit 125. When he was the ninth man out, Abell declared on 362. Somerset had a lead of 442 with more than a day to play, an advantage too great for Worcestershire. Despite a century from wicketkeeper Alex Milton on Championship debut, the hosts could not chase down their target. Jamie Overton picked up another four wickets as they were bowled out for 301. The win meant Somerset had jumped ahead of Nottinghamshire in the table, although their progress was bittersweet as Surrey had beaten Notts to maintain their lead at the top.

After the group stage of the Twenty20 Blast ended, the Championship run-in began. Somerset's first game of the all-important period was a tricky one with Essex visiting the County Ground. The match started well for the hosts as 95 from Trescothick and 70 from Abell gave them a solid foundation, but they were unable to build on that as they slipped from 285/5 to 324 all out. Nevertheless, it was still a decent score and one that looked a lot better once Essex were bowled out for 191. Jamie Overton was again the pick of the bowlers with three wickets. Looking to set a big target, the hosts struggled to build partnerships. Byrom was the only player to score more than 30 as they battled on a turning pitch. Harmer made the most of the conditions to pick up a four-for and restrict Somerset to 202. That still meant a lead of 335, however. Another win looked likely.

Yet Essex showed why they were champions. They remained unbeaten at the end of the third day with the score on 147/1. But Somerset's patience eventually paid off. After Leach dismissed Browne for 86, the spinner began to chip away. He finished the innings with 8-85 – his best figures in first-class cricket to date – to bowl the champions out for 290 and win the match by 45 runs. 'I have had some low times this season with two injuries and they make days like this all the sweeter,' said Leach, who had not played for England that summer. 'It's the best I have bowled because I needed to be patient on that pitch to get my rewards. During the days when I was injured, I kept telling myself there was a lot of Championship cricket still to be played. Now I can't wait for the remaining games.'

Despite the win, Somerset were still 32 points behind Surrey after they defeated Lancashire at the Oval. Unlike their previous victories, this one was much narrower. Needing 271 to win, Lancashire were bowled out for 264. Morkel had a six-for and Surrey had a six-run win. They could sense a first Championship title in 16 years. Time was running out for Somerset, but they had to keep going. Their next fixture was against Yorkshire at Headingley. After losing Trescothick and Byrom early on, they began to pile up the runs. Half-centuries from Azhar, Hildreth, Davies and Gregory gave them a big first innings total of 399. The hosts were also in fine form with the bat. Tom Kolher-Cadmore shared a 173-run partnership with Andrew Hodd to post 320 and get them back into the match. The pick of the bowlers was Davey, who claimed his maiden five-for in first-class cricket.

The match then began to swing in Yorkshire's favour as three quick wickets saw Somerset slip to 29/3. But Abell was not giving up without a fight. Batting alongside Hildreth and Gregory, who both scored half-centuries, he hit an unbeaten 132 to give his side a big lead. They were all out for 339 – 418 runs ahead – and late wickets on the third evening left Yorkshire languishing on 8/2. A home win looked unlikely. Despite some resistance from New Zealand captain Kane Williamson, four wickets apiece for Gregory and Jamie Overton helped them bowl Yorkshire out for 194 and secure a big win.

But again, Somerset's celebrations were muted. The day before, Surrey had smashed Nottinghamshire by an innings and 125 runs at the Oval to secure a seventh straight Championship win. Neither Surrey nor Somerset were blinking in the race for the title. Everything would change, however, during two extraordinary days of cricket. In early September, Lancashire, struggling to survive near the bottom of the table, travelled to Taunton. After winning the toss and electing to bat, the visitors struggled on a turning pitch. Only Alex Davies managed to score 20 as they were bowled out for 99, with Leach taking five wickets. Yet Lancashire had expected a spin-friendly surface and selected Keshav Maharaj, one of the world's best spinners. The South African got them back into the match with four wickets, helping to restrict the hosts to 192. If it had not been for Gregory's unbeaten 64, they would have barely had a lead.

Another two wickets fell before the day ended as Leach dismissed Davies for six and nightwatchman Matt Parkinson for a duck. Twenty-two wickets had fallen on the first day – and people were asking questions about the pitch. 'I am not worried about any possible penalty over the pitch because our last-wicket pair put on nearly 60 and showed what could be done on it,' said a defiant Kerr at the close. 'Jack Leach claimed five first-innings wickets, but he would be the first to admit he didn't bowl that well and there was some very poor batting by both sides ... I was very disappointed with the way we batted because there was the opportunity to establish a very big lead. I have not spoken to the cricket liaison officer and probably won't do so until the end of the game, but I don't foresee a problem.'

Somerset were later warned by the ECB's Cricket Discipline Committee after an investigation concluded the pitch should be marked as 'below average'. 'They are treading a very fine line,' warned the committee, who were not afraid to impose a points deduction. Meanwhile at Chelmsford, Surrey had made a good start against Essex, closing the day on 256/4. The champions-elect showed no signs of slipping up, but Somerset kept fighting and started the second day well. Craig Overton picked up three wickets before Leach did the rest. He finished with figures of 7-74 as Lancashire crumbled to 170. It left Somerset needing 78 to win – a tricky target considering Maharaj's form and the state of the pitch. And their chase started terribly. Former England seamer Graham Onions dismissed Trescothick and Azhar for ducks before Maharaj took charge. He picked up three quick wickets as they slipped to 37/6. Victory now seemed unlikely for the hosts, but Gregory, helped by Bess, revived their hopes. They put on 19 crucial runs for the seventh wicket before Gregory fell for 12, leaving Bess to continue the charge. He moved the score up to 77 before Maharaj had him stumped on 19.

As Leach made his way to the middle as Somerset's No.11, he aimed to score the most important single of his career to date. He had been in this situation before. In 2016 he and Groenewald put on 31 for the last wicket to guide them to an unlikely victory against Surrey. But that match was much earlier in the campaign. This was a season-defining moment – and Leach could not deliver. He was dismissed by Maharaj without adding to the total. For the first time in 15 years, a Championship match had ended in a tie. And, with Surrey enforcing the follow-on at Chelmsford after bowling Essex out for 126, Somerset's title hopes were all but over. Surrey went on to beat Essex by ten wickets to make it eight consecutive wins. A win over bottom-of-the-table Worcestershire in their next match would seal the title. It all looked academic. 'Whatever happens, the result is a huge blow to our hopes of winning the title,' said a dejected Hurry after the match. 'There is so much riding on every game and that's what makes today so disappointing.'

Somerset's last chance of overtaking Surrey – albeit very slim – was against relegation-threatened Hampshire at Southampton. And they struggled to cope with the brilliance of Hampshire's two South Africans. Kyle Abbott, who prematurely called time on his international career to join Hampshire on a Kolpak deal, showed his class with a five-for, and his compatriot Dale Steyn, one of the greatest fast bowlers to grace the international arena, took three wickets as the visitors were bowled out for 106. Somerset's attack did themselves justice in response, restricting Hampshire to 142/9 at the end of the first day. And there was some hope over at Worcester as the hosts had finished the day on 288/6. 'The wicket had a lot in it for the seamers and there was a lot of movement,' said Davey after the first day. 'They have an attack full of international quality, who made it difficult for us. They haven't got a big lead at the moment, so we need to come back in the morning and take that last wicket very quickly.'

They took that final wicket just six runs into the second day to bowl Hampshire out for 148. As they were just 42 runs behind, there was every chance Somerset could force their way back into the match. But they could not handle Steyn and Abbott. They took four and six wickets respectively as the visitors were bowled out for 116, Trescothick the last man to fall for 50. Craig Overton tried his best to turn the tide, but Hampshire coasted to victory. A six-wicket win boosted their survival hopes and meant that Surrey could secure the title at Worcester. 'It was a very interesting game,' said Abell after the match. 'We had a short game last week as well and this wasn't too different. Full credit to their bowlers, I thought they were outstanding. They asked a lot of questions throughout the game and we weren't up to it. Special mention for Tres today, he passed 26,000 runs and gave us a sniff, but it wasn't to be.'

Over at New Road, Surrey had enjoyed a much better day. They bowled Worcestershire out for 336 and Burns had scored an unbeaten 103 to leave them needing to avoid defeat to win the title. The next day they were bowled out for 268, but recovered well to dismiss their opponents for 203, with Morkel getting another five-for. On the final day, Surrey got the 272 runs they needed to win the match by three wickets and clinch the title. It meant another year of waiting for Somerset, although they could not be too dejected by the result with a big day out at Edgbaston just around the corner.

* * * * *

Somerset's semi-final opponents at Finals Day were Sussex, arguably the most talented Twenty20 team in the land. Phil Salt, Laurie Evans and Luke Wright were all capable of scoring at an alarming rate. And their attack was even better. Chris Jordan, Tymal Mills and Danny Briggs were all England internationals and Jofra Archer, one of the most exciting fast bowlers in white-ball cricket, was available for selection. Somerset could just be thankful that Rashid

Khan, the No.1 ranked Twenty20 bowler in international cricket, had finished his stint at Sussex. Yet they still had a chance of pulling off a shock. It was a proud day for Gregory, who was captaining his boyhood club at Finals Day. 'I've learned a lot throughout the competition,' he said before the semi-final. 'And I'm lucky there are some very experienced guys around me to help with that. It's been really nice to have that [responsibility] put on me.'

It was also a day to remember for Myburgh, his last as a professional cricketer. The 37-year-old had called time on his career and was desperate to bow out with a trophy. 'To the fans; playing in front of you has been an absolute pleasure and the energy you give to the boys on the field is something special,' wrote Myburgh in an emotional open letter. 'I would love to leave you with the special gift of a trophy at the end of this season and will do my best to assist the squad in bringing back the Twenty20 Blast trophy.'

But it was not meant to be. Having been so prolific throughout the tournament, Jamie Overton endured a nightmare semi-final. He conceded 50 runs from his three overs before he was taken out of the attack by Gregory, who did not fare much better. He leaked 49 from his four overs as Sussex finished on 202/8. Although they dismissed Salt and Evans quite cheaply, Somerset had struggled to keep Wright in check as he made 92 off 53 balls. It was always going to be a tough chase considering the quality of Sussex's attack. Myburgh's career was ended by Archer as he was dismissed for 22 following a valiant effort. Davies, Trego and others struggled to deal with the pace of the Sussex attack and when Abell was dismissed for 48 in the 15th over, the game was all but done. Somerset's innings ended on 167/8 and Sussex had secured a place in the final, where they would lose to Worcestershire. 'You've got to take your hats off to them,' admitted Gregory. 'Wrighty played brilliantly … I'm sure we'll all sit down and have a beer with Johann Myburgh tonight. He's been a fantastic player for us and he's one of the genuinely nice guys you want to have around.'

Not only did the defeat signal the end of Myburgh's career, but it also signalled the end of Somerset's hopes for a trophy in 2018. Nevertheless, a young team had performed brilliantly throughout the tournament and were gaining more experience with each boundary they hit. After reaching the semi-finals of the One-Day Cup in 2016 and the quarter-finals of both white-ball competitions the following summer, it was obvious they were getting closer to lifting silverware. Success was not far away.

* * * * *

There were only two Championship matches left in the 2018 season. Somerset's penultimate fixture was against Surrey. And the champions showed why they were the best team in England. Half-centuries from Burns, Mark Stoneman and Jason Roy were followed by an effortless century from Elgar on his return to Taunton. His 110 was the standout performance as Surrey made 485. The first ball of Somerset's innings demonstrated the difference between the two teams; Trescothick was bowled for a golden duck by Morkel. They were bowled out for 146 and forced to follow on. They showed some fight in the second innings, despite Trescothick again falling to Morkel to complete his pair. Azhar and Hildreth both passed 50 as they ended the penultimate day on 168/3. Then some bizarre weather got them out of trouble. A storm blew the covers off and damaged the wicket, meaning the match could not be completed. Somerset's blushes were spared, although it was obvious which side deserved to win. 'It was very windy and I am sure that Somerset haven't done this on purpose,' said Alec Stewart, Surrey's director of cricket. 'But we were trying to win a game and make it ten on the bounce. Whatever happened, we were well ahead, so it's a massive frustration.'

Not only had Surrey failed to win a tenth straight match, but they would fall short in their bid to complete the season unbeaten as Essex inflicted a one-wicket defeat at the Oval in the summer's televised finale. For Somerset, their season concluded at Trent Bridge. And the first day of the match was one to remember for the visitors. Trescothick made 71 and Hildreth hit 137. The following morning, they went on to post a solid first-innings score of 463. In reply Nottinghamshire struggled against their seamers. Craig Overton picked up four wickets, Gregory took three and Abell, much to the surprise of the crowd, dismissed Luke Fletcher, Matt Carter and Harry Gurney in consecutive balls to claim a hat-trick and finish Nottinghamshire's innings on 133. The hosts fought back as they followed on, but as the second day finished, they were 115/3 and staring at an innings defeat. 'It happened very quickly and is a bit of a blur but there was a little bit of swing and I tried to bowl in a decent area,' said Abell as he discussed his hat-trick at the close. 'I've got the ball and will keep it because it's probably the only time this will happen. I'm going to savour it.'

The following morning, Somerset finished the job. Nottinghamshire were bowled out for 184 as Craig Overton emulated his skipper by dismissing Ben Slater, Samit Patel and Riki Wessels to complete a hat-trick of his own. They had won by an innings and 146 runs to finish second in Division One. It capped off a good season for the club. They were competitive in the One-Day Cup, reached Finals Day in the Twenty20 Blast and had won seven matches in the Championship – the most they had achieved since they won Division Two in 2007. Various individuals had developed their game. Bartlett had scored his maiden first-class century, Bess had made his Test debut, Jamie Overton was the third-highest wicket-taker in the Twenty20 Blast, Gregory had proven himself as a captain, Banton had made his first-class debut and Abell had recorded his highest tally for first-class runs in a season – not to mention his breakthrough as a seamer. After the despair of 2017, this young team were now showing what they were capable of.

And for Kerr, that is what 2018 was all about. 'For me, it's all part of a journey,' he said, commenting on his first season in charge. 'I was naturally a bit nervous and apprehensive going into it. I'd done well in the roles that I'd held previously at the club, but you're never quite sure how you're going to handle it because until you've walked in someone's shoes, you never fully appreciate what the role entails. I knew how talented the group of players were, but it's about galvanising them and making sure that they work for each other. And we had a great leader in Tom Abell. But again, that doesn't guarantee you any success … You sensed a nucleus of players really working for each other. They started to demonstrate some resilience and were winning games from situations where previously, we may not have done. And you could see them growing as a side. We fell away towards the end and Surrey were the deserved winners, but I think that was a real stepping stone in our foundations in terms of people really believing we were on the cusp of doing something special.'

Somerset's second-place position meant they had finished as runners-up in ten tournaments since winning the Twenty20 Cup in 2005. Although they were improving each year in all formats, the failure of their predecessors to win finals and crucial Championship matches weighed heavy on their shoulders. The press still referred to them as the 'perennial bridesmaids' of English cricket, even though only Trego, Hildreth and Trescothick remained from the side they had built a decade earlier. They had the talent, now they needed the trophy. It was time for Somerset to condemn their recent failures to history.

2019

The Sweetest Victory

AFTER BEING well beaten to the Championship title by Surrey the summer before, Somerset were keen to improve their squad ahead of the 2019 season. Their biggest signing was Jack Brooks from Yorkshire. The seamer had been a key part of Yorkshire's title-winning campaigns in 2014 and 2015, taking 133 Championship wickets during those successful years. Although he was now 34, his 51 Championship wickets at an average of 28.03 in 2018 suggested he was as prolific as ever. 'I'm extremely excited to be joining Somerset at a time when they are building a special team capable of challenging for trophies,' said Brooks on signing. 'When I met Andy Hurry, Jason Kerr, Tom Abell and Andrew Cornish [the chief executive] I was impressed straightaway with their vision for the team and club. Their togetherness and desire reminded me a lot of Yorkshire when I joined them.'

It was a big coup for the club, who were concerned about losing some of their best players to England. 'There is a heavy schedule of international cricket next summer and we could lose one or more of our pace bowlers to England call-ups,' said Hurry. Many of their young guns had blossomed into fine internationals. Jack Leach had forced his way back into England's plans during a brilliant tour of Sri Lanka, where he took 18 Test wickets at 21.38 as they secured a 3-0 series win. Leach was now challenging Moeen Ali to be England's first-choice spinner and he would no longer be automatically available for Somerset. And Dom Bess was in a similar situation. While he managed only 16 first-class wickets in 2018 and had slipped down the international pecking order, he was still in England's plans. Thanks to their commitment to producing turning pitches, Somerset had supplied two international spinners for the national team.

Yet England were also interested in their seamers. Craig Overton had been given his ODI debut against Australia in 2018 and remained on England's longlist of bowling options. His brother Jamie and Lewis Gregory were also involved in the set-up, both representing the Lions during the previous winter. And there was always a chance that James Hildreth could finally be given a call-up, although his chances were becoming slimmer with each passing summer. Despite needing to safeguard against call-ups, they did not make any other permanent signings. They were continuing to put their faith in youth, with Peter Trego and Max Waller opting to sign white-ball-only deals. The decision not to give Trego a full contract was not surprising considering he had made just two Championship appearances in 2018. With numerous seamers emerging, such as Abell, he was deemed surplus to requirements. 'Although it's sad to bring the curtain down on part of my playing career, I feel I've given absolutely everything I have to offer to Somerset in Championship cricket,' said Trego when the news broke. 'I've loved every minute of wearing the whites for Somerset … I still have plenty more to achieve in a Somerset shirt and I'm delighted to still be a Somerset player.'

Although they had lost a few players from their Championship roster, Somerset did make a top overseas signing. Azhar Ali, after his late flourish the summer before, had agreed to come back. 'The supporters were excellent and I look forward to seeing everyone again next year,' said Azhar on re-signing. With Abell's young team improving and Azhar and Brooks adding plenty of quality and experience to the ranks, Somerset were looking like title contenders. *The Cricketer*'s Huw Turbervill and James Coyne predicted they would again push Surrey for the title, while *The Guardian*'s Ali Martin thought they would be crowned winners. *The Telegraph*'s Scyld Berry was also very complimentary, saying they were 'better-placed' to challenge in 2019. With the media hyping up Somerset's chances for the first time in a long while, the Taunton faithful remained expectant. It promised to be an exciting season.

* * * * *

Somerset's opening Championship match was against Kent at Taunton. Opening alongside Trescothick, now aged 43, was Azhar. But neither of them lasted very long as they struggled to build on starts. It was a new position for Azhar, who had been promoted to allow Hildreth to come in at No.3. With England captain Joe Root committed to batting at No.4, Hildreth moved up the order to try and claim a Test spot. 'I'm going up to three this year to maybe tell them I am still around,' said Hildreth on the eve of the season. 'It's probably quite unlikely with the guys they like to pick and who's on their radar, but the hunger is still there. At Somerset, we needed someone to move up to three or open … We had a chat about England, about their top order not firing and about how they potentially needed a No.3. That also gives the younger batsmen at Somerset the chance to come in at five and six rather than being chucked in at three as we have done in previous years.'

Yet his promotion did not work against Kent as he fell to Mitchell Claydon for 27. Abell fared slightly better in Hildreth's old spot, making 49, but that was as good as it got for Somerset. They were bowled out for 171 during a poor opening day. They did fight back, however. Like the hosts, Kent's batsmen made starts, but struggled to deal with Somerset's four-man pace attack of Craig Overton, Gregory, Brooks and Josh Davey. They were bowled out for 209 to leave the game hanging in the balance. It quickly, and literally, swung back in Kent's favour as Somerset were reduced to 17/3. Darren Stevens, Kent's 42-year-old all-rounder, was irresistible as he swung the ball through the Taunton air to dismiss Trescothick and Hildreth.

He went on to pick up a third wicket, but not before a man who was born after he had made his Championship debut in 1997 added 63 runs. George Bartlett, batting at No.7, played a brilliant counter-attacking innings to get Somerset back into the match. He was supported by Craig Overton's 28 and Brooks's unbeaten 35 as they reached 243. The hosts, with a lead of 205, now had something to bowl at. Sean Dickson, Heino Kuhn and Matt Renshaw, who was hitting centuries for Somerset 12 months earlier, were all dismissed without scoring as Kent slipped to 93/8. An unbeaten 43 from Stevens threatened to snatch the result away from Somerset, but he ran out of partners. They were bowled out for 131 as Gregory claimed a five-for. The hosts had turned the tide at Taunton to start their campaign with a win.

Their next match was against Nottinghamshire at Trent Bridge, which on paper seemed like a tough fixture. Nottinghamshire's top order had posted two solid scores during their draw against Yorkshire the previous week and, with Stuart Broad leading the attack, they were also a threat with the ball. And they were highly tipped by the media, expected to challenge Surrey, Essex and Somerset for the title. Yet they failed to repeat their batting exploits. They were bowled out for 263 as Gregory picked up another six wickets. In reply Somerset's top three all departed within the first 15 overs to leave them struggling on 36/3. But it was just a temporary blip as Abell and Bartlett produced a stunning 223-run partnership. They both made centuries to help Somerset reach 403. It was now up to Leach, playing in his first match of the season, to spin them to victory. He picked up a six-for as the hosts were bowled out for 126. They had hammered Nottinghamshire by an innings and 14 runs. It was a brilliant day for Leach, who was making just his second first-class appearance since the Sri Lanka series. 'You want to be contributing to the team,' he said. 'The first couple of days in this match I felt like I hadn't, so I was desperate to contribute where I could, but the seamers had bowled brilliantly.'

Leach had worked his magic at Trent Bridge to make it two wins from two. It had been an excellent start to Somerset's Championship campaign as they sat clear at the top of the table. Leach and Gregory were taking wickets for fun and Abell and Bartlett were giving them plenty of runs to bowl at. They were looking like a very strong outfit and were showing why they were so highly rated by the press. Their bid for a maiden title was well and truly alive.

* * * * *

Somerset's good Championship form was curtailed as the One-Day Cup began in April, much earlier than usual. It was the last time a domestic 50-over tournament would conclude with a Lord's final, bringing an end to 56 years of history. In future, the final will be played at Trent Bridge to allow Lord's to stage the semi-finals and final of The Hundred – the ECB's controversial new city-based tournament – on the same day. Therefore, to win the One-Day Cup this year meant just a little bit more than usual. Unaware of what the future may hold, it was viewed as the last Lord's final – the last chance for a county captain to lift silverware at the Home of Cricket. All 18 clubs were keen to give it their best shot.

The return of white-ball cricket meant the return of Trego, fresh after not playing four-day matches. Yet he was not the star of the show in Somerset's opening match against Kent at Taunton. That was young Tom Banton, who scored his maiden professional century at the top of the order. It was a brutal display. He smashed 107 off 79 deliveries to get them off to the perfect start. From there, the runs kept coming. Half-centuries from Gregory and Craig Overton allowed them to post 358/9. It was always going to be hard for Kent to chase down such a total, but no one expected them to be bowled out for 94. Craig Overton picked up five wickets to share the limelight with Banton.

It was a tremendous start for Somerset and things only got better from there. Two days later at Sophia Gardens, they bowled Glamorgan out for 259 to claim a narrow two-run victory. It was an extraordinary match. The visitors, struggling on 161/7, were only able to add those extra 100 runs thanks to an unbeaten 41 from Craig Overton and some useful knocks from Tim Groenewald and Davey. They then began to hammer home their advantage. Excellent opening spells from Davey and Craig Overton reduced Glamorgan to 21/5. At that point, the game looked done and dusted. But David Lloyd and Graham Wagg mounted a recovery. They put on 99 for the seventh wicket to bring Glamorgan back into the match. When Wagg fell for 62, the points seemed destined for Taunton again. But then Lukas Carey, the No.10, showed some more fight. He almost dragged Glamorgan over the line, falling just short of the target on 39 as Roelof van der Merwe saved the day. 'There's a ruthlessness in the side that we're creating now and even in situations where we're chasing the game, we're fighting for each other and we're getting through,' said Craig Overton afterwards.

Somerset followed it up with convincing wins against Sussex and Essex before things began to get tricky. They suffered defeats against Gloucestershire, Middlesex and Hampshire to leave their hopes hanging in the balance. If they wanted to progress, they had to beat Surrey at Taunton. They started the match well, restricting the visitors to 289/9. Craig Overton picked up three wickets and his brother Jamie finished with a four-for. In reply half-centuries from Bartlett and Banton, as well as 93 from Hildreth, was enough to get them over the line with five wickets and 26 balls remaining. 'I was disappointed not to see the job through, but it's always nice to score runs that help the team win,' said Hildreth. 'We were out of form with three successive defeats and that created a bit of added tension in the dressing-room. We needed to remind ourselves that we had won six games on the trot in the Championship and the cup before the three defeats and you don't become a bad team overnight.'

That win secured third place in the South Group and a quarter-final clash with Worcestershire at New Road. Somerset, batting first, made a blistering start as Banton scored his second century of the tournament. He was beginning to establish himself in domestic cricket. Despite no one else passing 50, runs flowed throughout the innings as they closed on 337/8. That was always going to be a tough total to catch, but Worcestershire remained in the contest until Abell made a surprise bowling decision. He brought Azhar on to bowl some leg-spin and he ended up taking five wickets as they were bowled out for 190. 'The way Bants played up front was outstanding,' said Abell. 'He is very capable of that and there were good contributions around him ... Then Azhar gets five wickets at the end. He's a great team man first and foremost and we're delighted for him.'

The team that stood between Somerset and Lord's was Nottinghamshire, who automatically qualified for the semi-finals after finishing top of the North Group. They were an excellent team, winning the tournament two years earlier. Yet their skipper, Steven Mullaney, made a misjudgement by putting Somerset in to bat. Banton carried on his good form with a half-century, Azhar made 72 and Trego hit 73. By the time the latter was dismissed for the sixth wicket, they had 252 runs to their name with more than ten overs remaining. In the end, they were dismissed for 337. With Alex Hales coming in at No.3, Notts certainly had enough quality to win the match. Hales had just been dropped from

England's World Cup squad for an off-field incident, not for his form.

Craig Overton, however, did not let Hales perform. He dismissed him for 54 before van der Merwe took the crucial wickets of Ben Duckett and Samit Patel to all but end their chances. Nottinghamshire were dismissed for 222 inside 39 overs to seal a big win. 'It means everything to lead the side through to a Lord's final,' said Abell. 'It will be such a special day ... I'm just so proud of the team, the squad and the coaching staff. I feel we are peaking at the right time and probably peaked in the quarter-final and semi-final, which is great with Lord's in mind. We got off to a fantastic start today, and we felt it was a really good score. They bowled well at the death, but I thought we were good in all three disciplines. It was obviously a big moment in the game once Hales got out, but there was still Moores and Mullaney to come at that stage and we were desperate to make sure they didn't come back into the game.'

Just 13 days after their win at Trent Bridge, Somerset travelled to Lord's for the final. Their opponents were Hampshire, the defending champions. They had enjoyed an excellent tournament, finishing top of the South Group and comfortably beating Lancashire by four wickets in the semi-final. And they had a superb team. Fidel Edwards and Kyle Abbott were former international bowlers, Sam Northeast was as classy as Hildreth in the middle order and Rilee Rossouw had scored three ODI centuries for South Africa. Yet they were missing two key players. Captain James Vince and all-rounder Liam Dawson had both been named in England's World Cup squad and, despite the tournament not yet beginning, were barred from playing in the final by the ICC. They instead played in a warm-up match against Australia, which took place at Southampton.

Their absence was a huge boost for Somerset, who were hoping to finally win silverware. Since they won the Twenty20 Cup in 2005, they had lost five finals and had finished as runners-up in five other tournaments. Yet Hurry was confident they could break that sequence, paving the way for more trophies to be added to their cabinet. 'Our aspirations are to win all three competitions,' he said. 'Once you win the first trophy you can look to build on that. And on our day, we are unbeatable ... I am convinced that any team who draws us in a knockout competition fears us and I'm sure Hampshire will be feeling that way, even though they are a very good side themselves.'

One player who was desperate to win the final was Trego. Although Hildreth and Trescothick had experienced all those near misses with him, they were both part of the team that won the Twenty20 Cup in 2005. Trego did not re-join the club until the following season, meaning the only trophy he had won as a Somerset player was the Division Two title in 2007. At 37, it seemed as if this might be his last chance to win a major honour. 'I don't believe in form in finals, it's just purely the team who turns up on the day,' he said before the match. 'There are so many things that go on before a final – the pressure, the media ... I suppose a few days out from a final you start thinking about the game, probably a little bit more than you should do. I try to set my mind to try and block out a lot of those things and be as consistent as I can be on the day. I know people say you've got to threat it like any other game, but I think people who say that haven't played in a big final.'

Thankfully for Trego, his nerves would have been eased as Somerset started the match well. Davey picked up two early wickets and Hampshire struggled to score runs against their seam attack. Their big hope was the aggressive Rossouw, who scored 125 off 114 balls to win last year's final. But he was dismissed by Jamie Overton for 28 just as he was getting into the game. James Fuller and Northeast, who was captaining the side in Vince's absence, both made half-centuries to keep their hopes alive, but they only reached 244/8. While it may not have been a huge score, it was still a competitive total and one that had the potential to condemn Somerset to another final defeat. But that did not happen. An excellent half-century from Banton and an unbeaten 69 from Hildreth secured, at long last, a trophy for Somerset.

And it was fitting that Hildreth hit the winning runs. He had been there throughout their entire journey, scoring the winning runs against Lancashire in the 2005 Twenty20 Cup Final and doing the same at Lord's. He had experienced every painful moment they had been through, missing out on Championship glory in 2010 at the last minute, losing three consecutive Twenty20 finals and enduring all those painful defeats at Lord's. 'I'm so glad we got over the line today,' he said. 'I'm really pleased for the boys, especially the young lads, some of their first experiences of being in a final. And to come away with the right result is great for them and hopefully a platform for us to kick on.'

Trego was also delighted. 'When you experience many decent years as a player you realise they were great times, but nobody at the club was satisfied,' wrote Trego in the December 2019 issue of *The Cricketer*. 'We wanted silverware sometimes so badly it affected my sleep. I know this will sound selfish, but I was damned if I was going to finish my time at the club without a trophy. I'd won overseas with Central Districts, but I wanted that feeling with all my best mates ... We had our moment. My long-standing team-mate James Hildreth and I could finally stop looking at our 20 runners-up medals we both had in our drawers at home and finally parade around Lord's with a trophy. What a game, what a day and certainly my proudest in a Somerset shirt.'

Although it was not the elusive Championship title they had been searching for, it was still a huge moment for Somerset. For so long, they had been described as the bridesmaids of English cricket, playing a starring role in so many ceremonies but never walking up the aisle first. But their victory at Lord's had ousted that belief. It was a huge relief for the team. 'It was like, "Wow, we won!"' continued Hildreth in his post-match interview. 'It was quite bizarre, but it was great, we've been bridesmaids for so many years. We've all seen the support in the stands, they come around everywhere with us. We've got the best support in the country, so it's great to do it for them.'

As Hildreth said, it was a day Somerset fans will remember for years to come. Although they had enjoyed watching many talented cricketers during recent years, the one thing they really wanted was a trophy. At one point, making the trip to Lord's or Edgbaston for a final was an annual pilgrimage, one which always ended in defeat. But at long last, they were able to celebrate a Somerset victory. Hurry recognises this – and how the triumph can inspire the squad and the next generation to keep succeeding. 'Whether you were a supporter or whether you were a player or whether you were a member of staff, people were crying because it meant so much,' explained Hurry. 'And that's because people work so hard. What's important is, whatever you're looking to achieve in life, you need to get some kind of reward at the end of it. It keeps you motivated. And I think one of the frustrations I had about us being second so many times was we never got the reward for all the hard work we did. This provided us with an opportunity to get that reward. It fuels us now to be even better. And what it also does is fuels the next generation. The next Tom Abell or the next Tom Banton is out there watching this group of players be successful. It's inspiring them. And then we can identify them, get them into the academy, provide opportunities and then they go on to play for England – how good is that?'

Paul van Meekeren also recognises how important that win was, although he appreciates there is still a lot of work to do to consistently win silverware. 'I think it brought a lot of relief to the members and to a few of the senior guys who have been in so many finals and kept losing them,' he said. 'But I think it's all about the Championship. Somerset is one of the most successful clubs, always competing for trophies but hardly winning them. It's always that last hurdle that seems to stop the team from winning trophies. I've seen over the last few years these rankings, where they get the form and stuff. I think Somerset are the No.1 ranked team in the country, but somehow, when they get to that final or semi-final they just get beaten on the day. The talent is there, but there might be something that's stopping them from winning those must-win games.'

Alex Barrow, however, believes the win could be the start of something special. 'A massive moment for them was winning the One-Day Cup. And that's because there have been so many seconds. I've been in changing-rooms in Championship cricket where we've been second, like in 2012, and it's been like, "We could have won this, but we haven't." And it was the same with one-day cricket and Twenty20 cricket where we've missed an opportunity. You only have to look at the boards in the Long Room to know how many times you've come second. But that doesn't always tell the full story. I wasn't involved, but the game against Lancashire when we tied chasing 70-odd [in 2018]. It's moments like that where you think, "We've missed a trick there" … You look at Tregs and Hildy, who have been involved in so many of those. To finally get their hands on a trophy is really significant. But also the youngsters who were involved in that, to know what it's like to win a trophy.'

One man who will savour it for years to come is Kerr. 'It was fantastic,' he said. 'The more time passes, the fonder the memories get. We had cricket to play not long after it, so I think that initial sense of relief and what it meant to the people in Somerset and the south-west, that was very obvious … It was good because I think it's about building belief in people and it's about building confidence. When you win and you actually see it through in a competition and take the trophy home, it's huge for everyone who has invested time within the club. It builds belief in people that actually a lot of what we're doing leads to success. And then it's how you improve on that to make sure you have sustained success … It's important we build on that now.'

Another former player who was delighted to see them win was Johann Myburgh. 'When I was playing, I always felt we were getting close,' he said. 'I desperately would have loved to have played in a Lord's final. I know if you ask any of the other guys, I kept on telling them, "Come on guys, I don't have many years left, we've got to get to Lord's!" So when they got there, quite a few of them messaged me, which was a nice touch, saying, "We got there, sorry it was a year late!" But I just believed that with so many talented players that are becoming mature cricketers, they were always going to head in one direction – if they had good leadership. And with Tom Abell and Lewis, they certainly do have that. Jason and Andy have done a great job since taking over and that combination is a very good one for the club. With Tom and Lewis leading and keeping what the squad is about, you're going to get the best out of these guys as human beings and, therefore, they'll play good cricket.'

After so many near misses, Somerset's victory at Lord's was one of the greatest in their history. Not only had it erased all those second-place finishes from short-term memory, but it had given Abell's ambitious team their first taste of silverware. While it was crucial for them to achieve this so early in their careers, it was also important to win a trophy early in the season. Although they had been the initial pacesetters in the Championship, there were still plenty of matches to go, as well as the Twenty20 Blast. Winning the One-Day Cup had given them the confidence to go and achieve something special in 2019. Pundits were beginning to believe they could emulate Warwickshire's treble-winning season in 1994 and, most importantly, win a maiden Championship title. 'We set out at the start of the season to win all three competitions and this was just the first one that came along,' said Abell after winning the match, aware the sky was the limit.

* * * * *

Before the One-Day Cup Final, Somerset had two Championship fixtures to play. The first was against Surrey at Taunton. With eight internationals in their team, it was always going to be tough to overcome the defending champions. And so it proved. Rory Burns, fresh from making his England debut during the winter, scored a century, as did Dean Elgar. There were also half-centuries from Mark Stoneman and Rikki Clarke as they scored 380. In reply the hosts were equally as impressive with the bat. Hildreth made his first big score since his promotion to No.3. His 90 was followed by an unbeaten century from Gregory, batting freely with the tail to get them up to 398. At this point there was hope of a home win. But Burns quickly quashed that with a crucial 78. A half-century from young Will Jacks also added to their frustration before rain finished proceedings. Although the match had ended in a draw, it was still an encouraging performance from Somerset. They had gone toe-to-toe with the defending champions, a team who had outclassed them the summer before. It was a sign of how much they had matured. 'We wanted to show we are a match for the team who won the title last summer and I felt we did that in all respects,' said Hurry after the match. 'It is a measure of the progress we have made.'

Somerset's next game was again at home, this time against Warwickshire. The opening day was another tough one for Trescothick as his poor form continued. After making scores of ten, five, ten and four in his first three Championship games of the season, he was dismissed for just five this time. In fairness to him his colleagues also struggled. If it were not for Davey's 36 and the 47 extras the visitors leaked, their score of 209 would have looked even more below-par. But Warwickshire did not fare much better. Five wickets for Craig Overton was a particular highlight as they were dismissed for 135. In their second innings the hosts battled again. Another high score of 36, this time from Craig Overton, was as good as it got for them as the medium pace of Liam Norwell picked up seven wickets.

Although they had added only another 164 runs, their lead of 238 looked considerable with batsmen struggling to make runs. Sam Hain tried his best to chase down the target with an unbeaten 92, but he eventually ran out of partners. Gregory's four-for ended their innings on 189 as Somerset claimed another Championship win. It was the perfect way to prepare for a Lord's final. 'We were getting a little twitchy the closer they got, but we still had plenty of runs on the board in the context of the game,' admitted Abell. 'We felt we had the situation under control and I would always back our bowling attack in that situation. Sam Hain played fantastically well to give them a chance, but we're really pleased to get over the line.'

A week after their Lord's win, Somerset travelled to Woodbridge Road in Guildford for the return match against Surrey. Although they were reduced to 35/3 on the opening morning, the visitors enjoyed a decent first innings. A century from George Bartlett helped them score 344. They then consolidated their advantage with the ball. Burns and Elgar, who both made centuries at Taunton a few weeks beforehand, were dismissed for two and one respectively as Surrey were bowled out for 231. Their blushes were spared thanks to an 81-run partnership from Ben Foakes and Ryan Patel. Despite their poor performance with the bat, the hosts fought back with the ball. Although Hildreth made

64, five wickets from seamer Matt Dunn restricted them to 153. With Surrey needing 267 to win, it was game on. And for a while, it seemed as if they would reach their target. A strong finish on the third day saw them close on 99/2 and in control. But the following morning, three quick wickets from Brooks turned the match back in Somerset's favour. His colleagues joined in the fun to dismiss Surrey for 164. They had dethroned the defending champions in their own parish. 'I just could not be prouder of the boys,' said Abell. 'This was a massive win for us. Surrey had eight Test players in their team and after the third day I would probably have preferred to be in their position.'

That win allowed Somerset to return to the top of the table ahead of their next match against Kent. Kerr had a big decision to make before play began at Canterbury. Trescothick had endured a poor start to the season, scoring just 86 runs at 10.75. With Abell willing to open, Azhar fully fit after missing the Surrey win with a chest infection and Banton in good form following his excellent one-day campaign, he was struggling to find room for Trescothick. 'While no one admires Tres more as a player and a person, my philosophy has always been that the greater good of the team goes before any other consideration,' said Kerr before the match. 'No one is more aware of his poor form than Marcus himself. He works so hard at his game, as well as remaining a real leader for us in the dressing-room. He was caught behind off his hip in the second innings at Guildford and that is the sort of thing that happens when you are struggling.'

Trescothick was omitted and never played first-class cricket again. With Somerset challenging for a maiden Championship, they could not afford to be sentimental.

They had to pick the best team available because one of the few things more important than Trescothick's legacy was that elusive success. And Trescothick knew this. He knew the end had come at long last, announcing his retirement just a few weeks later. 'I'm extremely grateful for all the support that I've received throughout this remarkable journey,' he said as the news broke. 'I've been discussing my future with the club and my family for a while and we felt that now was the appropriate time to make this announcement in order for both the club and I to put plans in place ... 27 years is a long time, but it's gone incredibly quickly. I consider myself very fortunate to have had the opportunity to do something that I love for that length of time ... This club, the members and the supporters mean so much to me. There are so many memories that I will cherish forever, and the club will always hold a truly special place in my heart.'

The brilliance of Trescothick was summed up by the flood of tributes that came in as he confirmed his retirement. The people of Taunton, his colleagues and the biggest names in English cricket, such as Michael Vaughan, Kevin Pietersen and Nasser Hussain, all paid tribute to him. 'I feel it's a sad day for cricket,' said James Anderson on the radio after hearing Trescothick's decision. 'He's been an amazing servant to England and Somerset. I am privileged to have played alongside him. I honestly think he had the potential to be the top England run-scorer of all time in both ODIs and Tests. He was that good. It's been an incredible career to play for as long as he has and with the quality he has. It's an amazing achievement. As a person and a team-mate, he was really special.'

And that is a crucial part of understanding Trescothick's genius. He was an incredible player, a naturally gifted left-hander who played with elegance and humility. But more importantly, he was – and remains – a great person. He inspired many youngsters as they came through Somerset's academy, including those who emerged almost 20 years ago, such as Hildreth and Arul Suppiah, and those who are just making their way in professional cricket, such as Banton and Bartlett. 'Growing up, watching him play for England, watching him play for Somerset and then going into the same changing-room with him was quite surreal,' said Barrow. 'But anybody who knows him will know he's just a fantastic bloke. He's very welcoming and very friendly. He's 40-odd years old and thinks he's 20 still! He's just enthusiastic, loves a joke. He's incredibly dedicated; trains very well. Tres is obviously top of the list of the players I have played with.'

While Trescothick's dismissal by Morkel at Guildford marked the end of his first-class career, the end of Somerset's campaign was still a long way away. After an excellent start to the season, their hopes were high heading into the match against Kent. But unfortunately, bad weather had descended on the British Isles. Rain had washed out the opening day at Canterbury and South Africa's World Cup match against West Indies at Southampton. The bad weather continued to wreak havoc on the World Cup during the next three days, with two matches being abandoned. It also disrupted Championship cricket, with games between Nottinghamshire and Hampshire and Surrey and Yorkshire ending in draws. But as rain fell around the country, play was possible at Canterbury. And the action was enthralling. Kent were dismissed for 139 in 41 overs as Gregory continued his good form with six wickets.

Somerset were just as poor with the bat. They could have been embarrassed by the hosts if it had not been for

Banton's 63, a crucial knock that got them up to 169 and gave them a precious lead of 30. Yet the day's play was not finished there. England hopefuls Zak Crawley and Joe Denly were dismissed before the close, meaning 22 wickets had fallen at Canterbury during a remarkable day of cricket. 'It was fast-forward cricket,' said Gregory at the close. 'We just tried to hit the pitch hard, hit the seam and there was enough happening for wickets to tumble. With the weather that's been around over the last few days the pitch was slightly juicy and helping the bowlers and, if I'm honest, there was a little bit of ordinary batting in there as well.'

No play was possible on the third day, but the rain did clear, allowing the game to conclude. Somerset wasted no time in ending Kent's second innings. Gregory finished with figures of 11-53 in the match as they were bowled out for 59. Abell and his opening partner Azhar then quickly got the 30 runs required – taking just 24 minutes – to make it five wins from six Championship matches. 'We still felt there was plenty of time left in the game despite losing so much to rain and once again our bowling attack proved just how good they are,' Abell said. 'The boys really took the onus this morning and bowled fantastically well. To dismiss them for 59 was testament to that group. Lewis will take the plaudits for getting 11 in the match, and rightly so, he was magnificent. But they all work so well together, I'm so lucky as a captain to have those four guys running in for me.'

Somerset's next game was at Chelmsford. After losing to Hampshire by an innings and 87 runs in their first match of the season, Essex had put a brilliant run together. They had won three of their past five Championship matches, losing none. Bowling first, the visitors struggled to dismiss Alastair Cook. The former England opener, who was available for Essex all summer following his retirement from international cricket, showed his class with a solid 80 in difficult batting conditions. It was a crucial knock that helped Essex post a competitive 216. In reply Somerset struggled to build partnerships. Azhar, Hildreth, Banton, Davies, Groenewald and Brooks were all dismissed for single figures as they made just 131. Jamie Porter, who had been named PCA Young Player of the Year and County Championship Player of the Year when they last won the title in 2017, picked up a five-for. The seamers continued to dominate as Essex's second innings began. Gregory and Groenewald took five wickets each as they collapsed from 163/5 to 183 all out. Cook again was the difference, scoring 47 precious runs in this low-scoring match.

To win Somerset needed 269. Their chase began poorly, losing Abell to the second ball of the innings. Azhar quickly followed, before a 39-run partnership between Hildreth and Banton steadied the ship. Gregory then made 40, but that was as good as it got. Porter picked up another four wickets as they were bowled out for 117. 'We were completely outplayed this week and didn't deserve anything,' admitted Abell. 'There were always good balls out there, but Alastair Cook scored 127 and, in the context of the match, that was massive. We couldn't quite do that with the bat … There have been times when we haven't been at our best this season when we've shown that fight and character to wrestle back the momentum. But we didn't do it this week.'

The result was a huge turning point in the season. For the first 12 weeks, Somerset had been the dominant force. Many were starting to believe it would finally be their year. But their defeat at Chelmsford ended their unbeaten record and, more importantly, meant that Essex were now just 13 points behind them. And they had a fabulous team. Along with Cook and Porter, they had accomplished internationals in Ravi Bopara, Ryan ten Doeschate, Simon Harmer and Peter Siddle. They also had two excellent youngsters in Sam Cook and Dan Lawrence. Essex had plenty of quality and momentum, yet Somerset could not be discouraged. A few days later they were back in Championship action, facing Hampshire at Taunton. After winning the toss and electing to bat, Abell and Hildreth put on a 178-run partnership for the second wicket. When they fell for 82 and 105 respectively, the runs continued to flow, thanks to Banton and Bartlett, who both made half-centuries. At 401/5, they were soaring towards a big total. But then came a collapse. They added just seven more runs as Abbott took the final three wickets to finish with a six-for.

Hampshire's response started poorly as Jamie Overton picked up two early wickets, but 55 from Ajinkya Rahane and a century from stand-in skipper Northeast brought them back into the match. More runs down the order helped them reach 349. Somerset's second innings began with a 128-run partnership between Abell and Azhar, who both fell short of three figures. When they were dismissed, Banton came in and added 70 to increase their lead. More runs followed and before the end of the third day, they had declared on 358/8. With a notional target of 418, it would have been wise for the visitors to try and bat out the match, but wickets soon began to tumble. They quickly found themselves 28/4 and, although Northeast and Fuller offered some resistance by sticking around together for nearly 18 overs, they never recovered. Their innings came to an end on 104 to complete a big win for Somerset. It was the perfect comeback. 'Once again our bowlers have performed fantastically well, as they have been doing all season,' said Abell. 'Of course, we can't avoid thinking about that first ever title because so much is written and spoken about it, but it's for the supporters and media to get excited. We will continue to look no further ahead than the next game.'

It was the perfect time to be playing Nottinghamshire, who had failed to win a Championship match all season. Making just his second first-class appearance for Somerset in 2019 was Bess, who had been on loan at Yorkshire in the Championship. Now, he was back at Taunton and producing the goods, hitting a half-century to help them post 326. He was batting alongside Davies, who top-scored with 74. Bess then left Nottinghamshire in a spin, taking five wickets to bowl them out for 241. They were going well, reaching 201/2 before Leach took the wicket of Jake Libby to trigger a collapse. The visitors fought back through their two spinners. Liam Patterson-White, a 20-year-old making his debut, and Ravi Ashwin, India's first-choice Test spinner, both claimed five-fors as eight batsmen failed to reach double figures. Only an unbeaten 65 from Azhar helped them post a below-par total of 169, but with a lead of 254 and Leach and Bess in their side, they were confident of victory. Leach used the spinning conditions to pick up four wickets as Notts were dismissed for 122. 'It was probably our most complete performance of the season,' said a delighted Kerr. 'When we are under pressure this season, we find ways of wrestling back the initiative.'

The next match against Yorkshire at Headingley was Somerset's last in the Championship for more than a month as the Twenty20 Blast halted the red-ball season. It was crucial for them to win – or at least avoid defeat – if they wanted to maintain momentum. But they would have to get a result without Leach and Gregory, who were playing for England Lions against an Australian XI. Without them, they struggled to take wickets. Bess did pick up four, but not before Gary Ballance, Tom Kohler-Cadmore and Harry Brook all made centuries. The hosts scored 520 and things only got worse. Keshav Maharaj tore through Somerset's lower order to finish with figures of 7-52. They were bowled out for 196 with only Jamie Overton making a half-century. Yorkshire enforced the follow-on, but the visitors showed some resistance. A half-century from Abell in an 89-run partnership with Azhar boosted their spirits, yet it was short-lived. Although Banton made 63, they eventually surrendered on the fourth day for 251, ensuring an innings win for Yorkshire. 'We weren't good enough from day one and we paid the price for that,' said Abell afterwards. 'The reality is we've had a fantastic campaign up until now and there's still a huge amount to play for. It's a blip. We lost at Essex and bounced back really well from that result. We'll be looking to do the same again.'

But, with only one Championship match being played during the next eight weeks, that was easier said than done. Somerset's defeat to Yorkshire had allowed Essex to claim top spot in Division One after they had comprehensively beaten Warwickshire at Chelmsford. It was now five consecutive victories for England's leading side, who showed no signs of slowing down. If Somerset wanted to be crowned champions, they would have to match Essex's tremendous consistency. It was set to be a fascinating conclusion.

* * * * *

Somerset's Twenty20 campaign began with a trip to Sophia Gardens. It was a tough start, as David Lloyd and Colin

Ingram made half-centuries for Glamorgan. Most of the bowlers took a bit of stick, including Jerome Taylor. He was back at the club after his impressive spell in 2018 and was keen to take them to Finals Day again. 'There was a great atmosphere in the dressing-room and that showed out on the pitch,' said Taylor on re-joining. But it was not a good day for him as he conceded 39 runs from his four overs. Babar Azam, Somerset's other overseas player, enjoyed a much better evening. He scored 35 on debut as they chased down Glamorgan's score of 180/5 with 12 balls and eight wickets remaining. It was a great start for Babar, who was the ICC's No.1-ranked Twenty20 batsman. 'I am looking forward to the new challenge that playing Twenty20 cricket in England will bring,' he said when he signed. 'I have heard good things about Somerset from Azhar Ali and I want to play a part in the club winning matches. I know that Somerset will get good support and I hope that I can give them something to cheer about this year.'

Although Babar did well, the star of the show was Banton, who made a match-winning 64 off just 34 balls at the top of the order to carry on his excellent summer. More runs came for him in the next match against Kent, 28 to be precise, but it was a bad day for the team. They were bowled out for 124 and lost by 41 runs. Captaining the team that day was Abell after Gregory was called into the England squad for their Test match against Ireland, along with Leach. 'We're incredibly proud of both of them and it's a fantastic reward for their efforts,' said Kerr as the news broke. 'Lewis has had a fantastic summer so far and has built on what he achieved last year whilst Jack has been outstanding for us again and he was brilliant out in Sri Lanka for England before Christmas. Ultimately, they both really deserve this. We're an aspirational club and we want our players to go on and represent their country.'

Leach made a remarkable 92 at Lord's to help England nervously overcome Ireland. Although Gregory did not receive his Test cap, it was still testament to how far he had come since his first-class debut in 2011. His impressive rise was no surprise to Andy Walter, who coached Gregory during his time at Devon club Plympton. 'He joined us when he was eight because his brother came down to our club,' explained Walter. 'Straight from day one you could tell Lewis had something. But he's worked really hard for it. He was the one who, during the school holidays, would always be at the nets. From quite an early age, 13, 14, 15 years old, you could see that he was planning [to become a professional]. It's not something that was totally natural to him. I would say 75 per cent of it was natural, but the rest of it he's worked really hard for.'

Walter also knew he would become a leader. 'He always had the personality to become a captain. He was opening the batting for us at 14 in the Premier League. We had a very good captain at the time and Lewis was always asking him questions, "Why did you do that? Why did you do this?" He was always learning the game and watching what was going on. He's a very knowledgeable person and a very educated person as well. We always had the feeling once he had made it, he would be looking to take a leadership role … From our point of view, we're proud as punch for Lewis and I think his parents have to take a lot of credit for the travelling they did. He was always going to the academy et cetera and it's not five minutes up the road from Plymouth. They've made sure he's kept his feet firmly on the ground.'

Gregory's exclusion from the Test team meant he was available for Somerset's next game against Hampshire at the County Ground. Babar played brilliantly, but his unbeaten 95 was not good enough as the visitors reached their target of 173 with three balls remaining. And it did not get much better against Sussex, falling 13 runs short and losing Gregory to injury. He was ruled out for an indefinite period after suffering a stress injury in his foot. 'This is incredibly frustrating news for Lewis because he's having an outstanding season,' said head of science and medicine Jamie Thorpe. Yet Gregory was not missed in their next match against Surrey. An unbeaten 54 off just 19 deliveries from Eddie Byrom helped them chase down Surrey's 203 with eight balls to spare. They were humbled against Middlesex at Richmond, however, as one of the world's greatest batsmen played a sublime innings. AB de Villiers, playing in his maiden Twenty20 Blast campaign, hit 88 off 35 balls to set Somerset a difficult target of 216, one which they could not reach. They hit back with a blistering win against Essex, though, scoring 225 runs.

Somerset followed that up with victories against Hampshire and Kent, the latter being remembered for a 51-ball century from Banton. Defeats against Gloucestershire and Surrey hampered their hopes, although they did enjoy a 25-run win against Glamorgan. Going into the final match against Middlesex at Taunton, they needed to win to progress to the quarter-finals. With their opponents in the exact same situation, it was effectively a knockout fixture. 'We need to win, it's as simple as that,' said Kerr. 'Middlesex are a strong side and they pipped us in a competitive game at Richmond, so hopefully we can turn the tables and come out on top. Knowing that our future in the competition is in our own hands takes the pressure off a bit. It's a one-off game and the winner will be the team who plays better on the night.'

Somerset were handed a boost ahead of the match after Gregory was declared fit to bat, yet he was not required as Abell played an extraordinary innings. He smashed an unbeaten 101 off 47 deliveries to help them post 226/5. If Middlesex were to pull off a successful chase, it would be the highest in the history of the competition. It seemed as if the hosts were guaranteed to make the quarter-finals. But Middlesex started well. A useful knock of 41 from Dawid Malan kept them up with the required run-rate and de Villiers was scoring quickly until an outstanding piece of fielding got rid of him. After hammering the ball to cow corner, it looked like he had hit a flat maximum. But a leaping Waller plucked the ball out of the air with his right hand, before nonchalantly celebrating. The catch typified just how good Somerset are in the field. According to Darren Veness, they succeed because of their commitment to fitness. 'Whether they're still at the club or not, they pride themselves on their physicality,' he explained. 'And if you look at the fielding performances that Somerset are putting out now, they're outstanding. From a fitness point of view, that's where it stands out because the fitter you are, the smarter you are. It's less likely your brain is going to get fatigued if your body isn't fatigued.'

After Abell's century and Waller's catch, it seemed as if it might be Somerset's evening. But then came one of the great knocks from Eoin Morgan. After a cautious start, England's World Cup-winning captain decided to up the ante once de Villiers had gone. Finishing with eight sixes, he made 83 off 29 balls to win the match and drag his team into the next round. And it was not even close as they completed the record chase with three overs remaining. Yet that was as good as it got for Middlesex as they were knocked out in the quarter-finals. Essex went on to win the tournament by defeating defending champions Worcestershire in the final.

'Somerset played extremely well,' admitted Morgan after the match, 'but just not well enough.' It was a very disappointing way for their Twenty20 campaign to end, one which should have finished much later considering their batting exploits. Banton scored 549 runs in the tournament – second only to Babar, who made 29 more. Abell also came into his own as a Twenty20 player with an excellent century against Middlesex. But with the ball, they struggled as Taylor and Craig Overton both finished with economy rates of more than nine runs per over. They dearly missed Jamie Overton, their leading Twenty20 wicket-taker in 2018, who made only four appearances, as well as Gregory. 'The overriding emotion is disappointment,' said Abell after the Middlesex defeat. 'We have not finished the competition well. At times we've been really good, at others we've let ourselves down … We felt capable of achieving something special in this competition, but we didn't pull it off tonight. We're a young side and we will learn from this.'

And that much is true. With the emergence of Banton, Byrom and Abell, along with Gregory, Craig Overton and the quality overseas players they sign each summer, Somerset will have plenty of chances for Twenty20 success in the future. They just had to accept that 2019 was not going to be their year.

* * * * *

Although their Twenty20 hopes had been crushed by Morgan, Somerset were still fighting for the double.

Unfortunately, they were doing so without Azhar after he was recalled by Pakistan. 'After discussing this with Azhar, he felt that the team's needs should come before his and he has therefore agreed to return to Pakistan early,' said Kerr. Azhar's recall came just before they faced Warwickshire at Edgbaston in August, the only Championship match to take place during the Twenty20 Blast. After dismissing England hopeful Dom Sibley for a four-ball duck, Somerset's attack looked to dominate. Yet Will Rhodes and youngster Robert Yates dug in to put on 153 for the second wicket. Rhodes failed to reach three figures, falling on 82, but his 19-year-old partner recorded his maiden first-class century. At the end of the first day, Warwickshire were 303/4 and in control. But after a good night's sleep, the visitors fought back. They bowled Warwickshire out for 419 before Davies, promoted to open after Azhar's departure, scored a century. Although they were missing Azhar, his compatriot Babar was available for selection, but he failed to score as Oliver Hannon-Dalby dismissed him for a golden duck. An unbeaten 52 from Bess got them up to 308 to avoid the follow-on.

Somerset were more than 100 runs behind entering the second innings as Warwickshire made a good start. At 107/4, it seemed as if they were taking the game away from their guests. But a revival, led by Abell's four wickets, kept their score down. They were bowled out for 146 to give Somerset a chance of victory. Their chase started nervously as they slipped to 49/3. Thankfully, Babar was on hand to rectify his poor first innings. He hit 40 to steady the ship before Banton made 66 to get them closer to the target. Bartlett and Bess then put together a match-winning partnership of 88 to secure an unlikely win. 'It was always going to be tricky chasing on the final day,' admitted Abell. 'The way

Georgie Bartlett played this afternoon was mature beyond his years and showed a great temperament, alongside Dom Bess, who had a great game. We've got guys who can bat all the way down.'

Yet it was a bittersweet result as Essex had bowled Kent out for 40 to win at Canterbury. Somerset remained the chasers going into the final three games of the summer. The first of those came at Taunton as Yorkshire made the journey south. Making his debut was Murali Vijay, who had been signed to replace Azhar. The 35-year-old had spent the previous summer playing for Essex and touring England with India. On paper, he was a brilliant signing for the run-in. 'Somerset have an excellent reputation and I am looking forward to being a part of what they are trying to achieve,' said Vijay. But he made a poor start after being dismissed for seven in his maiden innings. Abell's 66 and Jamie Overton's 40 offered some resistance against Maharaj, who was back at Yorkshire for the final few games of the season, but it was the only defence they had as he finished with five wickets to restrict them to 199.

Somerset performed better with the ball, running through Yorkshire to bowl them out for 103. The wicket of Ballance proved to be crucial as his dismissal for 35 triggered a collapse from 70/2. It was an excellent display of fast bowling from Davey, who finished with figures of 3-30. Their second innings started poorly as Vijay failed to add to the total. Davies was also dismissed early on, but half-centuries for Abell and Hildreth, who had returned to No.4 following his Ashes snub by England, increased their lead. Decent knocks of 43, 47 and 39 from Banton, Bartlett and Gregory respectively saw them reach an unassailable lead of 425. The only Yorkshire player who could be happy with his performance was Maharaj as he dismissed another five batsmen. It brought his first-class tally against Somerset up to 31, with those wickets coming at an average of 13.06.

After gaining such an advantage, victory was only a matter of time. Yorkshire offered little resistance as they were bowled out for 127, ensuring a Somerset victory inside three days. And the good news did not stop there. Essex had drawn against Warwickshire at Edgbaston to allow Somerset to return to the top of the table with two games remaining. 'I am not mentioning the title in the dressing-room,' said Kerr. 'Of course, we are aware of people outside discussing it because it would be a first for the club and has long been described as the Holy Grail. But we want to continue focusing on one game at a time and going about things the way we have done all season. We try to build pressure and, if you do it for long enough, the rewards will come.'

The equation was now simple. Somerset needed to beat Hampshire and avoid defeat against Essex to win the title. And they took a huge step towards doing that after reducing Hampshire to 24/5. They continued to take wickets in Southampton, but a counter-attacking century from Dawson helped the home team reach 196. The visitors had let a big opportunity slip and they regretted it dearly when Abbott was given the ball. He dismissed nine batsmen as they were bowled out for 142. Somerset were now behind in the match and things only got worse when Vince, Hampshire's other World Cup winner, came to the crease. As wickets fell around him, he made 142 to give them a lead of 280. While Somerset were still in the game, a draw was now out of the equation and a defeat looked likely. They made a good start, as Vijay and Davies put on 86 for the first wicket. But when Vijay fell for 29, Abbott crushed their hopes. He took another eight wickets, finishing with 17 in the match to bowl them out for 144. 'Hats off to Kyle Abbott,' said Abell. 'He was unbelievable throughout the game. He got the ball tailing and we needed to adapt better as batters … There is a huge amount of excitement around Somerset cricket at the moment and we are desperate to deliver the Championship. This week hasn't gone our way, but we have a good opportunity next week.'

It was a huge result. Essex had beaten Surrey by an innings and 40 runs to move 12 points clear at the top going into the final match of the season. Although Somerset's fate was still in their own hands, they needed to beat Essex at Taunton to win the title. The 2017 champions were undefeated since the first match of the season and the forecast was not ideal, with rain threatening to fall throughout. And Somerset had a tough decision to make when it came to the pitch. In 2018, they had received a final warning from the ECB after they, not for the first time, found the pitch to be 'below average'. They had been told a points deduction would be implemented if another poor pitch was prepared, which in layman's terms is one which spins excessively. With Leach back from playing a vital role in England's drawn Ashes series against Australia, they could not afford to be overzealous in their preparations. Nevertheless, Abell was still excited for the biggest first-class match of his career to date. 'We've got one game to go and it's a must-win,' he said during the build-up. 'As disappointing as defeat by Hampshire was, we've got to put it behind us and be in the best frame of mind possible.'

The match did not start well, however. Rain restricted play to fewer than 28 overs on the first day as Somerset reached 75/4. The pitch was already beginning to turn significantly, with Essex spinner Harmer picking up two wickets. Although the hosts were taking a huge gamble by preparing a spinning wicket, they had to take that risk considering the poor weather forecast. A good batting track would not produce a result. 'The pitch is doing plenty for the bowlers already, with some seam movement and spin,' said Hildreth, who made 32 before succumbing to Harmer, at the close of play. 'I can't see it getting any easier to bat on, although you can never quite be sure at Taunton. Knowing there was some bad weather forecast, we had to make sure of producing a result wicket. Anything above 200 will be a good score.'

And Somerset were able to reach Hildreth's target. They were bowled out for 203, but only managed to post that after van der Merwe and Leach added 59 for the last wicket. Unsurprisingly, Harmer was the pick of the bowlers, finishing with a five-for. Essex openers Cook and Nick Browne were able to negotiate the final 11 overs of the day before rain restricted proceedings again. At the halfway stage, Essex were firmly in the driving seat. 'It's quite tough when Harmer is in that kind of mood and bowling well,' said van der Merwe at the close. 'There were men around the bat, so I tried to put a bit of pressure on him. We just have to be patient in the way we go about things, not worry too much about the scoreboard and land the ball in good areas.'

Somerset's patience did not pay off, however. The third day was completely washed out, leaving Essex on the verge of becoming champions again. 'We've put too much on the line, for too long a period to wave the white flag,' said a defiant Hurry at the close, not willing to give up on their dream just yet. When the final day came, the weather had improved significantly. But the hosts needed a miracle and with Cook at the top of the order, it was always going to be tough. He made a half-century to move Essex to 102/1 and within touching distance of the title. Yet Somerset kept going. A collapse, led by Leach's five wickets, saw the visitors dismissed for 141. With only an hour left to play, they decided to forfeit their second innings and set Essex a target of 63 to win, forcing them to bat out the last hour.

But the visitors did not succumb to the pressure. Browne and Cook saw off most of the hour before Westley came in to finish the job. Essex had got over the line and Somerset had been denied again – and this one was tough to take. They had led the Championship for a large part of the season and had won nine matches, which would have been enough to win the title in 2010, 2012 and 2016. 'We took it right down to the wire,' said a dejected but proud Abell after the match. 'That middle session gave us a chance to win the game, but it wasn't meant to be. To give ourselves that chance was an incredible effort. We're gutted, we were desperate to try to get over the line ... Over a Championship season, the best teams will always prevail so congratulations to Essex. It's been a good race at the top.'

It was also Trescothick's last chance to win the Championship as a player. He had to accept that it was not going to be, but as he walked off the County Ground to a standing ovation, it would have been the last thing on his mind. He had become a legend at the club and set the standard for future generations to follow. Rather than ponder on what could have been, it was time to enjoy everything he had achieved as a player with a few ciders. 'No words can do justice to what Tres has done for this team and for Somerset cricket as a whole,' added Abell. 'A phenomenal player but an even better person. It's a void that I don't think can be filled in the immediate future. But that's a challenge for us as younger players to try and step up and emulate what he has done.'

While Somerset gave Trescothick a fine send-off, Essex celebrated their double-winning season. After toasting their success long into the night, their skipper Ryan ten Doeschate woke up the next morning in the coach's office, still wearing his whites with Cook asleep on one shoulder and Westley on the other. Although he was elated with their triumph, he was also relieved to avoid defeat in difficult conditions. 'It was a weird one,' said ten Doeschate after the match, disappointed with the standard of the pitch. 'The weather kept pushing us back time-wise, and I felt by the latter stage of day three, we'd done enough. We knew the wicket was going to be horrendous, but we didn't know quite how bad … You literally felt that every ball was a challenge.'

And ten Doeschate was not the only person who was dissatisfied with the pitch. After various warnings, the ECB decided to punish Somerset. They will start the next Championship campaign on minus points and, if they are found guilty again in the future, will receive another penalty. As the Championship campaign did not happen in 2020 because of the Covid-19 pandemic, they may have to win one or two games more than their nearest competitors if they want to be champions in 2021. They were initially deducted 12 points, although that could change as the Championship has been restructured into three conferences ahead of the 2021 season. To put this into perspective, teams received 16 points for winning a Championship match in

2019, with up to eight bonus points available. They will also have to ponder whether they still want to encourage spin at the County Ground. It is effective thanks to Leach's quality, but their success is coming at a price.

That said, 2019 was still a season to remember. Although they had failed to progress in the Twenty20 Blast, they had finished second in the Championship and had convincingly won the One-Day Cup. For Kerr, it was a significant improvement on the previous year. 'I can think of numerous situations where we were behind the eight ball in games,' he said. 'In domestic cricket, you often see those games go with the team that's got the current advantage. And we actually managed to wrestle it back, numerous times. Lots of different people contributed throughout the year and again, that to me is a sign of people working together, playing well and, more importantly, building confidence in themselves and each other ... If we'd have played a full campaign this year [2020], it would have been fascinating to see how they would have gone.'

Their win against Hampshire in the One-Day Cup Final will be vital as they look to compete during the next few years. They will be hoping to take inspiration from that win and not focus on the Championship result between the two at Southampton, when they let their position slip. With the Essex match coming just a week later, they would have known about the poor weather forecast and just how important that penultimate match was. It should have been a game that all-but secured their maiden Championship title. Instead, it became an occasion remembered for Abbott's record-equalling performance. If Somerset want to be successful in the future, they must win these all-important matches.

In July 2020, *The Cricketer* released a special issue which celebrated the last 50 years of county cricket. It included plenty of statistics to help summarise each decade. Hildreth was the highest run-scorer in the Championship during the 2010s, making nearly 10,000 runs, while Trescothick was fourth on the list. It also included the most successful teams in terms of trophies. Nottinghamshire, Warwickshire and Hampshire all finished with four pieces of silverware each, while Yorkshire and Essex had both won two Championships. And for all their hard work, Somerset had just one trophy to their name. According to *The Cricketer*'s criteria, they were the 11th most successful county of the decade. But in reality, they were one of the best in the land.

The team from Taunton had finished second in the Championship on five occasions. To put this into perspective, Yorkshire, the most successful Championship club in history with 33 titles, have only finished in the top two five times since 1970. To come so close on so many occasions in such a short space of time is a terrific achievement. They have also been competitive in Twenty20 cricket, reaching Finals Day five times between 2009 and 2018. And they performed well in one-day competitions, twice finishing as runners-up during the decade and winning the One-Day Cup in 2019. It is hard to deny that Somerset and their supporters have experienced the most disappointments during the last decade or so, yet they have also enjoyed the most excitement.

Somerset may not have won the Championship during the last decade and with each near miss, they are reminded of that. But would they trade all the drama, all the heartache and all the entertainment for one Championship-winning campaign and nine dull seasons? Not a chance.

Epilogue
Can Somerset Win the Championship during the 2020s?

IT IS the big question – can Somerset end their long wait and win the County Championship in the next decade? The victory in the 2019 One-Day Cup Final is seen as a pivotal point in the club's recent history. It was the moment when they shrugged off their 'bridesmaids' tag and confined their second-place finishes to history. And now, it would be easy to assume they can go on and win plenty of trophies, but we have been here before. In 2007, Somerset stormed to the Division Two title with ten Championship wins. That could have, and should have, inspired Justin Langer's emerging team to win silverware. Yet they won nothing. Will Tom Abell's side do the same? Will their greatest hour always be that famous day at Lord's? Or can they go on and create a dynasty? Can they become Somerset's greatest ever team? Can they win their maiden Championship title?

It was not meant to be in 2020 as the Covid-19 pandemic significantly reduced the season. It was not safe to start playing county cricket again until August and by that point, there was not enough time for a Championship campaign to be completed. It was replaced by the Bob Willis Trophy, a first-class competition named after the late, great England captain who passed away in December 2019. Somerset enjoyed an excellent start to the campaign, defeating Glamorgan by 289 runs. They followed that up with another big win against Northamptonshire – by 167 runs – before the weather denied them against Warwickshire. A 314-run win against Gloucestershire followed before they edged Worcestershire by 60 runs in their final match. They recorded 97 points in the group stage to secure their place in the final to be played over five days at Lord's in late September. Yet they were unable to repeat that success in the Twenty20 Blast. Nottinghamshire went on to win the only other domestic tournament in 2020 and Peter Trego, who was released at the end of the previous season by Somerset, was part of their triumphant side.

Somerset's opponents at Lord's were Essex. Almost a year on from their title decider at Taunton, the two sides were again facing each other in a season-defining contest. This time, however, the weather forecast was decent. A draw seemed unlikely. If it did end in a draw, the team with the highest first-innings score would win. Batting first, Somerset scored 301 thanks to a century from Eddie Byrom. But Essex fought back through Alastair Cook, who hit 172 to give them the all-important first-innings lead. They declared on 337/8 and despite Somerset hitting 272/7 to keep their hopes alive before declaring, the damage had been done. Essex saw out the fifth day on 179/6 to draw the match and win their third major first-class trophy in four years. 'Coming so close so many times, you certainly feel a first-class trophy is in touching distance,' said Abell afterwards. 'But playing the brand of cricket we have been in recent seasons, we're confident we'll come out on top sooner rather than later.'

Although Abell admitted the loss was 'disappointing' and it was another final defeat, Somerset were not competing for the Championship title. A win would have been nice, but Essex would have remained the defending champions even if the result had gone the other way. And it was a tight match, with many viewing the first-innings rule as unfair. It proved, along with the rest of the truncated 2020 season, that Somerset can continue to compete for silverware. One man who has absolute confidence in them is Chris Rogers. 'You've got this group of great young batsmen coming through that you have every right to be excited about,' he said. 'The likes of Tommy Abell and Banton and George Bartlett. You've got a side that is on the up. Sometimes I look at some of the other sides that have peaked a little bit. I think that the Yorkshire side under Jason Gillespie peaked and then they were all getting on a bit together and there was a big clean-out, whereas I reckon Somerset are just getting going. They have this potential. They still could be three, four years away from being at their best.'

The man who brought Rogers to the club and gave the likes of Abell, Craig Overton, Lewis Gregory and Jack Leach a proper chance in the first team also has complete faith in them. 'They've got a side together there that could be a side for the next six, seven years,' said Matt Maynard, who will be trying to stop them winning trophies as Glamorgan's head coach. 'With the talent there they will lose the odd player to England, but there's depth there. As long as they can keep all the players happy, I've no reason to think they can't win the Championship. They're a tight bunch, they've got the same goal and they've got two great leaders there, one in Tom Abell and the other one in Lewis Gregory.'

For Nick Compton, it is their quality and strength in depth that will get them over the line. 'I do think they can win the title,' he said. 'Championships are won by bowling attacks and a solid batting line-up. If you look at Somerset's bowling attack and some of the reserves they've got – and the age of those players – I think they've got as good of an opportunity now as ever … And I think it's like anything: once they get over the hurdle and win that first Championship, others will come. And that's probably what we found. Take away the Championship, we got to all those Twenty20 and one-day finals and we just couldn't get over the line. It was amazing how we performed in those finals. It was just like, "What is going on? We should be winning this game!" And I guess that just shows the pressure, we just weren't able to get that elusive victory. And I think when they do things will move forward.'

Steve Kirby agreed: 'There is no doubt in my mind the team will win that Championship at some stage. They're a really powerful side, they've got a lot of bases covered, they've got a work ethic and they're starting to see some young players kick on. As long as England don't nick too many of their players, I think Somerset have got a real good chance. What I look for in a Championship-winning side is the ability to take 20 wickets. They can do that now with both seam and spin bowling. But the one thing where you know you've got a team is when you're four or five down and you've got people like Roloef van der Merwe, Lewis Gregory and Craig Overton coming in. They've got an engine room in the batting order that can, somehow, get

CAN SOMERSET WIN THE CHAMPIONSHIP DURING THE 2020s?

350, 400. I really think Somerset are one of the strongest, if not the strongest, team out there.'

Somerset's biggest strength is their bowling. In 2019, Gregory, Leach, Craig Overton and Josh Davey all averaged 21.89 or under in the Championship. Gregory's figures were particularly impressive; 51 wickets at 15.76. Dave Stiff acknowledges this and believes it will be key to their success. 'Looking at all the sides that have won in recent years, obviously you have to score runs, but it tends to be teams where the bowlers have dominated,' he said. 'If you look back at the last few years with Essex, they've had Simon Harmer, Sam Cook and Jamie Porter. And when Yorkshire dominated for a couple of years, they had Jack Brooks and Ryan Sidebottom. The sides who have dominated have had two or three bowlers who have got 40, 50 or 60 wickets and are bowling sides out consistently to win matches.'

The batting, however, does need to improve. In that same Championship campaign, only Abell and George Bartlett averaged more than 30, while no one averaged more than 32. They suffered from not having a recognised opener with the likes of Abell, Tom Banton and Steven Davies usually filling the void. Their top six were constantly in flux, with no one, not even James Hildreth, having a solid position in the order. In comparison, Essex had four batsmen in their settled top order – Cook, Dan Lawrence, Tom Westley and Ravi Bopara – who averaged 36 or more. While most domestic red-ball cricket was played during the bowler-friendly months of April, May and September in 2019, Somerset must do better with the bat and ensure everyone knows their role if they want to win that coveted title.

Somerset's squad is much younger than it was a decade ago. The average age of the team that played the final

Championship match against Durham in 2010 was 29.27, but in 2019's equivalent against Essex, that figure dropped to 27.72. For Adam Dibble, this is what gives the current Somerset team the edge over his former colleagues. 'I think the difference between now and then is there's a younger core to the side,' he said. 'And there's five, six, seven years of that core remaining. Even Hildy, who's the old man of the team, still has another three or four years left in him if he can keep performing; he's definitely fit enough. I think there are fewer egos around. I think there's a better team spirit, looking out for each other and working hard for each other. Whereas before, there were too many people who were in it for themselves … I don't miss playing anymore, but I'm actually envious that I'm not around that kind of environment because it looks like a great atmosphere. I've got no doubt they will win more trophies.'

Michael Munday added: 'Somerset have got a little bit of stick, fairly or unfairly, for choking in finals and stuff like that. But in a 16-match league format, if you're the best team you've got a pretty good chance of winning … It feels as if they're doing something right, in terms of the academy and bringing players through. You would like to think that over the next three or four years – and it's harder to look any further than that – there's a structure in place and there are good players there who will win Championship games. In 2010 when we came very close to winning the Championship, the strength of the side was probably from abroad and other counties. If you look at now, particularly how we cast the net to Devon and have Overton and Gregory coming from the region and being the standout players in the side, I think that is a better place to be. Guys like Zander de Bruyn, for example, you get him but he's never going to play for eight years. I think he was there for three and then he was gone.'

There is a collective fearlessness ingrained within the current Somerset team, one which their youngsters, playing without the scars of previous failures, inspire. 'I'm not surprised at all that they've managed to build the team that you now see,' said Michael Bates. 'Lots of internationals, lots of potential internationals … With Jason Kerr as head coach and Andy Hurry, they've got some brilliant foundations to keep building and get better. And I think we're starting to see the results of that. I guess kind of like our Hampshire team: once you've got a taste of winning, once you know how to win competitions, there's really no stopping you … There's a great balance now between young talented cricketers coming through and, actually, a lot of those lads in the Somerset team are coming towards the peak of their career – 27, 28, 29, 30 years old. And I think they feel very passionately about the club, which is really important.'

Thanks to the outstanding structure in place at Somerset, that team should not grow old together. Although they have lost Dom Bess to Yorkshire and Jamie Overton to Surrey ahead of the 2021 season, new players are constantly coming through and trying to win a place in the first team. A fine example of this is Tom Lammonby, who made his first-class debut during the Bob Willis Trophy. Opening the batting, the 20-year-old from Exeter scored three centuries during the tournament, including an excellent 116 in the final. It was another glowing reference for their academy. 'The talent within Somerset and within the pathway of Somerset is exceptional,' said Paul van Meekeren. 'There's a young kid, Will Smeed, who was out with a shoulder injury last year. He scored a hundred in second-team cricket at 16 and Marcus Trescothick scored a hundred down the other end. He's one of those guys, but if you look throughout the last few years, Bartlett, Tom Banton now, all these guys coming through the ranks. It's incredible the depth that Somerset have in their pathway.'

Of all the ones to watch, Smeed is the player widely tipped to make the biggest impact. He made his professional debut during the 2020 Twenty20 Blast, scoring 82 in just his second appearance against Gloucestershire. And after his exploits in the second team alongside Trescothick, he is not far away from first-class cricket. 'He's had a couple of injury setbacks, but he is an absolutely amazing player,' said Phil Lewis of King's College. 'He's got a real four-day-game pedigree. He's destructive and can play Twenty20 as well as the best of them, but he's got great patience. He's an incredibly intelligent player, as well. Mix that with a highly competitive edge and a great technique, he's definitely going to be one to look out for. It's just a shame in what should have been a breakthrough season, it's all gone a bit pear-shaped because he's literally had no chance to show what he could do this year [in first-class cricket]. There's also a couple of other younger players in the academy that are coming through and look very strong ... It's very exciting.'

It is important not to underestimate the value of Somerset's coaching staff. In Andy Hurry and Jason Kerr, they have two brilliant coaches who understand exactly what the club needs and are executing their plan of producing international cricketers and creating a strong second team to perfection. But there is far more to Somerset's coaching structure. New academy director Steve Snell, who succeeded Kerr, knows the philosophy of the club, having played there for two years, and with Trescothick becoming the assistant coach, the players will continue to benefit from his influence. And because of their connections within the region, it would not be inappropriate to suggest they have dozens of coaches and scouts across the south-west looking to find their next international.

One of those people keeping an eye out for the next Trescothick is Alex Barrow. 'Culturally they're all very good,' he said. 'They're all buying into the same thing. And the skill level is undoubtedly there. They've found ways to win at Taunton, which was always a struggle through the 2010s and prior to that. They'll have to be careful because they're on a bit of a warning, but the pitch can still spin. They've still got quality spinners and they've got Lewis Goldworthy coming up as well. They'll win plenty of trophies, but the big one is the Championship. If you'd have said to me, "Do you think they would have won it in the last three years?" I would've said, "Yes." They've come very close and that's sometimes how sport goes. But I also think that in a league or a prolonged championship, the best team will always win. You can't get lucky with winning something like that. But there's definite quality in the playing side, the coaching side and the wider club. They'll win trophies.'

George Dockrell added: 'I think if you look at the make-up of the team, there's a great bunch of guys there. Jason Kerr was absolutely fantastic when I was there. He's someone who is not only a fantastic coach but is also a great guy and has so much respect from me and all of the guys from when we came through. And I think that's a huge part of it, that he's got a bunch of guys around him that he's helped get to where they are ... They've got all the pieces in the squad, from all aspects of the batting, seam bowling, spin bowling, plus winning games at home. I think they've shown in the last number of years that they've been consistently up there and I have no doubt they've got a great chance of winning the Championship in the foreseeable future.'

Yet there are no guarantees Somerset can win the Championship – as was demonstrated by how close they came in 2010. Although he does think they can be triumphant, Charl Willoughby remembers the pain of just missing out. 'They've got an amazing squad of players and I get down to watch them quite regularly,' said Willoughby. 'When we were good at Somerset, we were a little bit ahead of the pack. When I went to Essex, I realised how far ahead Somerset were in terms of discipline, fitness, structure – all that sort of stuff. Subsequently things have changed at Essex, and I think other teams have caught up with Somerset, so it's going to take a monumental effort to win the Championship – any Championship-winning season is a monumental effort. You need a lot of things to go your way; people not getting injured; having a lot of people in form. If someone does get injured, you need a youngster to come in and find his feet straight away. I do think they have the talent and ability. I think they have the leadership structure there, which is good.'

Willoughby also believes they made a mistake in letting Tim Groenewald leave. During his time at Somerset, Groenewald averaged under 30 with the ball in first-class cricket each summer. 'For me, losing Tim Groenewald is a bit of a blow,' he said. 'I think he is a consistent performer. He's not a world-beater, but he gets you the two or three wickets you need and gets some runs at the back end.

Players like him and Jack Brooks need to be fit and ready to go all the time. You need your three or four core bowlers to not get injured … If they do ever win it, I'm going to take a little bit of it with me. I poured some serious blood, sweat and tears to win it!'

Despite losing Groenewald, Somerset still have enough talented players to win the Championship. But whether they have the mental strength to be the best team throughout an entire summer remains to be seen. That is their biggest hurdle to overcome. 'The talent is there,' said van Meekeren. 'I think there's something missing in the squad. And it's not the talent or the X-factor, I think it's more things that bring teams together off the park. It's quite tough to put your finger on it. They are one of the fittest and most talented groups of players, but somehow they can't get across the line. They do everything right training wise, fitness wise, talent wise, but for me, if I were leading the club I'd be asking, "How can we win the game? Where do we go wrong?" … I would have done a few bits differently.'

Jim Allenby added: 'The team they've got now is the best squad in the country, by miles. I wrote something, somewhere, saying the Somerset squad is comfortably the best in the competition and I think their second team would win Division Two. England selections haven't hurt the team as much recently, so if they can keep their guys together and keep that mentality of playing for each other, then there's absolutely no doubt that Somerset should win not just one Championship, but should be the real dominant team for the next five to ten years because they've got some players there who haven't even reached their peak yet and are match-winning, international-quality players. I don't think it will be a skill or talent issue if they don't win it, it'll be to do with the approach and the mindset.'

Ultimately, most former Somerset players agree they have the talent and attitude to win the Championship. But they must maintain their desire for 14 matches. 'We were always blessed with a very talented squad,' noted Johann Myburgh. 'I made a statement when I retired that they were going to win a lot of trophies because all those players are extremely talented and are now at an age where they are going to be winning cricket matches regularly … You're going to be playing against other squads that are really good and want to win the Championship, so they have no right to do it because they're talented. They certainly have all the tools and it will be up to those guys whether they can pull together at very difficult moments within a season. If they can stand up and maybe eke out a draw or maybe squeeze over the line for a win, that's the small margins. It's not when you're playing well, it's when you're slightly off it and you can scrape something and get over the line.'

Arul Suppiah added: 'They've got a very exciting current side, young players and a mix of experienced players … On any given day, we can win a trophy – like we did in 2019. Whereas Championship cricket, it's more of a mindset. And I'm glad that the team is quite different [from red-ball to white-ball]. It's not a totally different team, but there are different bowlers and a different wicketkeeper. I think that can help because, for me, Championship cricket is ultimately the hardest; it's the most complex. Winning matches is really important, but actually what's more important is digging out in situations where you're in trouble and coming out with a draw, rather than losing.

And that's because those little things can boost the morale of the team.

'I'm not sure how Somerset are going to prepare the wickets. Obviously they've gone with spin, but now what do they do? Do they take that gamble again? That could play a part. But I definitely think in the next five years, I don't see why we can't win the Championship. You can have great players, but I always think of teams like New Zealand. They have one or two great players, but they play well as a team. I think that's what's needed in Championship cricket: that consistency and focus for the whole period of time. You can have great players come in and play one or two matches, but what's going to win you the Championship is the team and every squad player contributing.'

Although the views of all these former Somerset players matter, the most important opinions are those of Hurry and Kerr. When I asked them if they could win the Championship during the coming years, I expected a reserved response. I was worried they might even be annoyed by the question, tired of being asked whether they can deliver the ultimate prize. But they were bullish; confidently putting their faith in the squad. 'We've got to continue to have competition for places, that's the recipe for success,' said Hurry. 'You want guys who are frustrated in the second team because they're knocking out back-to-back hundreds against sides who are asking questions with the ball, but they can't get in the team because the first team is doing so well. The great thing about that is the first team can't rest on their laurels. We've got that competition, so I'm really excited about the next three to five years around what the club can achieve. We will continue to keep exposing players and provide those opportunities for them so we can accelerate their individual development.'

Kerr added: 'For me, the sky's the limit. They're an incredibly talented bunch. The number of players who are on the periphery of playing for England; the number of players who have been in the squads. Individually, in terms of their aspirations, they're starting to achieve those. And the challenge within that is making sure we've got players coming through behind who can sustain their skill levels and deliver and put pressure on those guys. I think that's really important for us to have sustained success. But also, if we keep the nucleus of those players together, I think the challenge with having more success is that people want more; they want more opportunities. And the challenge within that is trying to keep that side focused: a nucleus of players working to the same common goal.'

And ultimately, the responses of Hurry and Kerr tell you all you need to know. A decade ago, Somerset were a club that wanted to win every competition. Today, they are a club that can win every competition. And that is the big difference; that is why they have every chance of winning the Championship during the next decade. They need to improve in some arears, but thanks to the culture they have in place, one which the likes of Brian Rose, Langer, Hurry, Maynard, Kerr, Rogers, Trescothick and Abell all helped build, they have the right attitude, an abundance of talent and enough desire to win plenty of trophies. After years of being the bridesmaid, Somerset finally became the bride by winning the One-Day Cup in 2019. And during the coming years, there will be no divorce from success.

Appendix
Somerset during the 2010s

County Championship
Runners-up: 2010, 2012, 2016, 2018, 2019
Joint-most wins in Division One (54, shared
with Yorkshire)

One-Day Cup
Winners: 2019
Semi-finalists: 2016
Joint-most group stage wins (27, shared with
Yorkshire, Essex and Nottinghamshire)

ECB 40
Runners-up: 2010, 2011
Semi-finalists: 2013
Most group stage wins (33)

Twenty20 Cup
Runners-up: 2010, 2011
Semi-finalists: 2012, 2018

Champions League
Semi-finalists: 2011
The best performance by an English side in the
competition's history

About the Author

Thomas Blow is a writer from Sheffield, living in London. He has written for *The Cricketer*, *Late Tackle*, *World Soccer*, These Football Times, The Football Pink, *The Daily Telegraph* and *The Sun*. He studied history at Leeds Beckett University (BA) and the University of Sheffield (MA). His first book, *The Honorary Tyke*, was released in 2020 to critical acclaim.

Also available at all good book stores

9781785316395

9781785317224

9781785315053

9781785314865

9781785314377

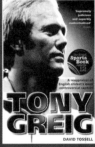

9781785313981

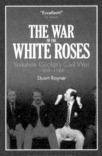

9781785314070

9781785313806

9781785317217